1916
Ireland's Easter Rising
Shots That Cracked an Empire

A COMPENDIUM
of
People, Places and Events

Frederick G. Fierch

HERITAGE BOOKS
2008

HERITAGE BOOKS
AN IMPRINT OF HERITAGE BOOKS, INC.

Books, CDs, and more—Worldwide

For our listing of thousands of titles see our website
at
www.HeritageBooks.com

Published 2008 by
HERITAGE BOOKS, INC.
Publishing Division
100 Railroad Ave. #104
Westminster, Maryland 21157

Copyright © 2008 Frederick G. Fierch

All rights reserved. No part of this book may be reproduced or transmitted in any form or by any means, electronic or mechanical, including photocopying, recording or by any information storage and retrieval system without written permission from the author, except for the inclusion of brief quotations in a review.

International Standard Book Numbers
Paperbound: 978-0-7884-4487-6
Clothbound: 978-0-7884-7193-3

POBLACHT NA H EIREANN.

THE PROVISIONAL GOVERNMENT
OF THE
IRISH REPUBLIC
TO THE PEOPLE OF IRELAND.

IRISHMEN AND IRISHWOMEN: In the name of God and of the dead generations from which she receives her old tradition of nationhood, Ireland, through us, summons her children to her flag and strikes for her freedom.

Having organised and trained her manhood through her secret revolutionary organisation, the Irish Republican Brotherhood, and through her open military organisations, the Irish Volunteers and the Irish Citizen Army, having patiently perfected her discipline, having resolutely waited for the right moment to reveal itself, she now seizes that moment, and, supported by her exiled children in America and by gallant allies in Europe, but relying in the first on her own strength, she strikes in full confidence of victory.

We declare the right of the people of Ireland to the ownership of Ireland, and to the unfettered control of Irish destinies, to be sovereign and indefeasible. The long usurpation of that right by a foreign people and government has not extinguished the right, nor can it ever be extinguished except by the destruction of the Irish people. In every generation the Irish people have asserted their right to national freedom and sovereignty; six times during the past three hundred years they have asserted it in arms. Standing on that fundamental right and again asserting it in arms in the face of the world, we hereby proclaim the Irish Republic as a Sovereign Independent State, and we pledge our lives and the lives of our comrades-in-arms to the cause of its freedom, of its welfare, and of its exaltation among the nations.

The Irish Republic is entitled to, and hereby claims, the allegiance of every Irishman and Irishwoman. The Republic guarantees religious and civil liberty, equal rights and equal opportunities to all its citizens, and declares its resolve to pursue the happiness and prosperity of the whole nation and of all its parts, cherishing all the children of the nation equally, and oblivious of the differences carefully fostered by an alien government, which have divided a minority from the majority in the past.

Until our arms have brought the opportune moment for the establishment of a permanent National Government, representative of the whole people of Ireland and elected by the suffrages of all her men and women, the Provisional Government, hereby constituted, will administer the civil and military affairs of the Republic in trust for the people.

We place the cause of the Irish Republic under the protection of the Most High God, Whose blessing we invoke upon our arms, and we pray that no one who serves that cause will dishonour it by cowardice, inhumanity, or rapine. In this supreme hour the Irish nation must, by its valour and discipline and by the readiness of its children to sacrifice themselves for the common good, prove itself worthy of the august destiny to which it is called.

Signed on Behalf of the Provisional Government,

THOMAS J. CLARKE.
SEAN Mac DIARMADA.   THOMAS MacDONAGH.
P. H. PEARSE.   EAMONN CEANNT.
JAMES CONNOLLY.   JOSEPH PLUNKETT.

Proclamation of the Republic of Ireland- April 24, 1916

Flag of the Irish Republic which flew over the GPO during the Easter Rising

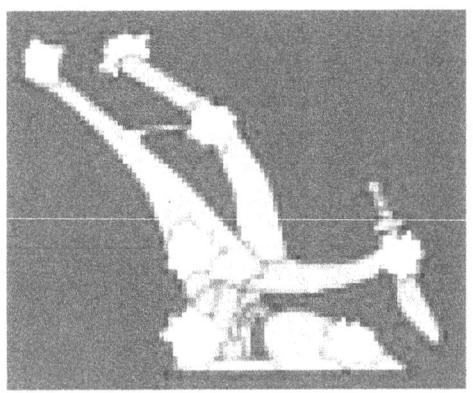

Flag: Citizen Army
Used during Easter Rising

To free, Irish people everywhere,
May the memory of Easter 1916
  give you pause to relish that freedom
  you have,

and,

To my wife, Gloria (McCauley) for
all the support during this project.

Table of Contents

List of Illustrations..	vii
Acknowledgements...	viii
Introduction...	ix
Prologue..	xi
Timelines...	1
General Map of Operations...............................	4
Organizations..	6
Personalities...	9
Synopsis- The Easter Rising.............................	33
Dublin: 1916 & Today......................................	44
Gravesites...	49
Casualties...	54
Destruction...	58
Court Martial Results......................................	62
Executions..	66

Book Reviews

The Capuchin Annual 1966	Fr. Henry	71
The Easter Rebellion	Max Caulfield	73
The Rising	Desmond Ryan	74
Witnesses	Annie Ryan	75
No Ordinary Women	Sinead McCoole	76
A Walk Through Rebel Dublin	Mick O'Farrell	77
The Women of 1916	Ruth Taillon	79
The Easter Rising	Foy & Barton	80
1916 Easter Rising	Tim Pat Coogan	81
Rebels	Peter deRosa	82
The Easter Rising	Richard Killeen	83
The Easter Rising	Kostick & Collins	84
Agony at Easter	Thomas Coffey	85
The 1916 Rising	Edward Purdon	86
Rebel Ireland	Sean McMahon	87
Easter 1916	Charles Townshend	88
Where's Where in Dublin	Joseph Connell	89
Desmond's Rising	Desmond Fitzgerald	90
The Irish Times: The 1916 Rising	Hegarty & O'Toole	91

"A Soldier's Song"	92
Joseph Plunkett & Grace Gifford	93
Escape from the GPO	100
The Death of the O'Rahilly	104
The Role of the Capuchin Friars	107
James Connolly as Military Commander	111
Cathal Brugha at South Dublin Union	114
The Murder of Francis Sheehy-Skeffington	116
Sir Roger Casement	118
Spirituality of the Rebel Leaders	120
Audio Tapes: Fr. Leonard Coughlin OFM Cap	123
Cumann na mBan	124
Countess Markievicz	126
The Battle of Mount Street Bridge	129
1966 Pearse Commemorative Coin	133
Postage Stamps & The Easter Rising	135
Movie Review "Michael Collins"	140
90th Anniversary Observance	142
Epilogue	145
Bibliography	146
Index	149

List of Photographs and Diagrams

Cover	National Library of Ireland- Online Exhibition "1916" (NLI-Ex)
Title Page	Courtesy- National Library of Ireland (NLI)
Proclamation	Courtesy Capuchin Archives (Cap Arch)
Flags	NLI
Page 4-5	author
Pages 9-22	NLI
Page 23	Cap Arch
Pages 24-32	NLI
Page 45	Cap Arch
Pages 46, 47b, 48t, 50	author
Pages 47t, 48b	NLI
Pages 51-53	Courtesy David Conway
Pages 67, 68, 70	author
Pages 93	O'Brien Press
Pages 95, 97	Irish Academic Press
Page 96	author
Page 97	NLI
Page 99	NLI
Pages 103-104	author
Page 106	NLI
Page 107-108	Cap Arch
Page 109-110	author
Page 113t	Cap Arch
Page 113b	NLI
Page 114	Cap Arch
Pages 116, 117, 118	NLI
Page 122	Cap Arch
Pages 125, 126, 127, 128	NLI
Page 131	Cap Arch
Page 133-134	www.wikipedia.com
Pages 135-139	An Post
Page 140	©Warner Bros.
Page 141	NLI-Ex
All Maps	NLI-Ex

Every effort has been made to insure that proper permission has been received from the copyright owner. Any omission was not intentional and please forward any claim to the author or publisher for proper consideration.

Acknowledgements

I am indebted to a number of people who assisted the preparation of this project, if not in a physically assistive nature, then in a source of encouragement. Of the former, Ms. Paddy Pender at the Capuchin Friary, Church Street, Dublin, never hesitated in offering assistance to my many questions. Fr. Leonard Coughlan, OFM Cap., lit the passion for the subject. The Capuchin Archives in Ireland readily gave permission to use their resources. In the preparation of the manuscript, my daughters, Reness DiCenso and Alexandra Peracciny offered invaluable suggestions for design and layout as well as the mundane chore of proofreading.

The encouragement aspect of the project was provided by Mr. J. Ed Lozaw (from the Phelan & Stenson families of Mountrath, Co. Laois), the greenest Irish-American in our area of New York State.

Introduction

It probably seems unnatural for a person with eight German grandparents to have a profound interest in a period of Irish History. The Easter Rising was sparked within me by a set of circumstances owing to the ancestors of my wife.

About four years ago, I discovered the graves of Patrick and Bridget (McKenna) McCauley in a local cemetery. They were the great, great grandparents of my wife and no one in her family was aware of those graves. Upon consulting their death certificates, I discovered that both of them had been born in Dublin in the 1830's.

A website for the Diocese of Dublin listed just nine city parishes in 1836, so a letter was written to each of them in the hope of discovering the home parish of the McCauley family, with visions of a journey to discover roots. All responded, but none of them was positive. A very nice reply was received from the parish office of Church and Halston Streets, the churches of St. Mary's of the Angels and St. Michan's.

In the midst of the genealogical effort, circumstances prevailed which would allow the two of us to receive the matrimonial sacrament. We decided that it would be most fitting if we could arrange this in Dublin at the parish of my wife's ancestors. I contacted St. Mary's of the Angels about a wedding (we selected that church because of their kindness during our initial contact and because we still did not know the original parish of the McCauley's) and a positive response was received. We went to Dublin in April, 2004, and the ceremony was completed. (On the day of the wedding, I was at the National Library of Ireland and learned that the parish I was seeking was St. Mary's of Haddington Road- that church played a role in the Easter Rising).

While at St. Mary's of the Angels, we were introduced to Fr. Leonard Coughlan, OFM Cap. At the time of our meeting, Fr. Leonard was ninety- two years old. I explained to him that I had begun research into the Easter Rising, and that I was well aware of the role played by the Capuchin Friars (and of the friary in which we were sitting) during Easter Week 1916. He explained to me that his earlier colleagues, Frs. Albert, Aloysius, Augustine, Columbus and Sebastian had administered to those executed at Kilmainham in May, 1916. He also gave me a series of audio tapes on which he relates the last hours of the prisoners as had been told to him by those mentioned above. Listening to those tapes inspired me to gain all of the information available relating to the Rising and embark upon an intense study.

While in Dublin, we visited Glasnevin Cemetery, Arbour Hill Cemetery, the General Post Office (GPO); we drove around the remains of Jacob's Biscuit Factory, the South Dublin Union, Mount Street Bridge, St. Stephen's Green and the College of Surgeons. And, of course, we spent a great deal of time on Church Street, between the area of the Four Courts and King Street North. As a historian, I was amazed to discover how much remained, how little was marked for the tourist, and what was available in print about the Easter Rising.

A fair question might be posed: Why again examine a topic which has been fully analyzed over the decades? Initially, my response would have been that most of the accounts are disjointed, or many things had been missing from one or the other work. Actually, everything is available for a thorough understanding of the event, however, nowhere is everything in one volume. I began to realize that I should not attempt to give another version of the Easter Rising, but that I should prepare a work to serve all: a guide to all available information, whether narratives, photographs, maps, biographies, gravesites, bibliographical information, book reviews and other caveats. In that manner, I would be serving a reader with a casual curiosity as well as a serious scholar.

To say that the Easter Rising is the seminal event of Irish History over the past several centuries, is perhaps overlooking the fact that it is but one part of a trilogy, played out by many of the same characters between 1916 and 1923. But the Rising itself has special significance in that it was a doomed enterprise led by a diverse trio, resulting in the resurrection of the Irish national soul.

Tom Clarke, the old Fenian, James Connolly, the staunch socialist, and Patrick Pearse, the school master imbued with the Gaelic spirit, united to ignite the spark which eventually brought the world's foremost imperial system to its knees. These three led a military exercise, though they were not soldiers. In a way, all three were dreamers, and because of that, none feared death in the pursuit of Irish nationhood. Their 'triumph of failure' gave impetus to the others: Arthur Griffith, Michael Collins, Eamonn deValera, etc.

Prologue

The Easter Rising of 1916 was an event doomed to failure from the very beginning. The primary leadership within the Military Council if the Irish Republican Brotherhood (IRB) had no illusions about chances for success. Their goal was multi-faceted: (1) Awaken the national spirit of the Irish people, both within and outside of the island, (2) Attack England when the country was most vulnerable i.e., The Great War had been bleeding England for two years and its outcome was very much in doubt by April, 1916, (3) Attempt to establish an Irish Republic which would be in place whenever a peace conference would settle World War I, thereby receiving *de facto* recognition, and (4) Show the world that the Irish people felt so passionately about their heritage and country that they were willing to battle the most powerful imperialistic nation on earth to achieve full independence and rid Ireland of 700 years of British rule.

There was a split within the leadership of the national movement as to the most prudent manner to achieve an independent Irish state. The commander of the Irish Volunteers, Eoin MacNeill, along with Bulmer Hobson and The O'Rahilly, felt that the Home Rule Bill which had been passed by the English Parliament in 1914 would guarantee independence. That statute, although passed into law, had been tabled for the duration of the war. The more militant members, Patrick Pearse, Thomas Clarke and Thomas MacDonagh knew from experience that the English could not be trusted and felt that a military confrontation with England, while that country was at its weakest, was the only method which would convince the British, and the world that the Irish were determined to achieve nationhood.

Another player in the preparation for the Easter Rising was Sir Roger Casement and his efforts to gain assistance from England's enemy, Imperial Germany. Casement had been a bureaucrat within the English Colonial Office and had achieved knighthood for his efforts in Africa. By 1914, he had retired and returned to Ireland. He had always expressed a desire to assist in the freedom of his homeland and began to lobby the IRB leadership to allow him to lead a mission to Germany. The purpose for his contact with the Germans was to gain armaments for the Rising and to recruit from among Irish prisoners of war; he wished to create a regiment which the Germans would transport back to Ireland to fight with the Volunteers. Along with these two tasks, Casement was also to gain recognition for the Republic of Ireland from the Germans once they had won the war.

Sir Roger did succeed in having the Germans send a ship with armaments to Ireland. That story, the voyage of the *Aud*, is amazing in itself, but suffice to say, the ship arrived off Fenit at the precise time scheduled as designated on its departure from Germany (sadly the date had been changed during the voyage, but there was no contact with the ship and the captain never knew of the changed date), but two days earlier than expected by the Volunteers. In those two days, the British captured the ship and the arms never reached the Volunteers.

The leadership of the IRB had been united about a rising at Easter, based upon the success of the arms shipment from Germany. At the last moment, MacNeill cancelled the rising which had been scheduled for Easter Sunday. The cancellation had been placed in the newspapers and the Volunteers who had prepared to muster full strength, stood down instead.

The Military Council leadership was stunned by the cancellation order. They had been deceiving MacNeill for months about their true intentions, but his order had caught them completely by surprise and left them with a dilemma. Would they forge ahead anyway, knowing that the German assistance was not forthcoming, and also that their ranks would be depleted by MacNeill's cancellation? Or, would they comply with the orders from their commander and await another window to strike?

At their meeting on Easter Sunday, Thomas Clarke wanted to go forward as scheduled on that day. The others were of the mind that they should analyze the situation to determine exactly what the cancellation order had done to their plans. It was decided that the rising would be postponed one day and that it would commence at noon on Easter Monday. To that end, a countermanding order was sent out from Dublin to every Volunteer unit throughout Ireland instructing the leaders to muster their men for the new date. By the time the message was received *and verified* the original formations planned for Sunday had dispersed and could not be reorganized by Easter Monday at 12:00.

On that fateful day, the four Dublin battalions of the Volunteers and Connolly's Citizen Army turned out at Liberty Hall and at Dolphin's Barn. Out of an original force of 4000 men, no more than 1200 were available.

At that point, the philosophical and practical questions began regarding the decision to continue with plans to battle the British Empire. Certainly Pearse, Clarke, Connolly and MacDonagh were well aware that militarily they had NO chance of success. Connolly had been quoted as saying that if they made it one day, the Rising would have been a worthwhile venture. What did they hope to gain from a folly of failure? They were well aware that if they survived the battle, they would surely be executed.

Patrick Pearse was a romantic who cherished things *Gaelic Irish*. As a poet and teacher, he was well prepared for his destiny as he saw it. To die for Ireland's freedom in dramatic fashion was his way of planting a permanent seed, the type of which previous attempts at self rule had not sustained.

Thomas Clarke was sixty-two years old at the time of the Rising. He had spent fifteen years in a British gaol for Fenian activities involving explosives. He was the primary impetus for the continuity of both Sinn Fein and the IRB. Clarke did not care if he survived the Rising as he stated that he could never return to a British jail, and that the current generations of Ireland had to be shown that courage to challenge the British Empire was the only method of attaining freedom. Thomas MacDonagh had become Thomas Clarke's disciple and was completely in accord with his feelings. It was MacDonagh who had developed most of the military dispositions and he was eager for the fight to begin.

James Connolly was an extreme socialist who led the ITGWU (workers union). When that labor union had been involved in the disastrous Lockout of 1913, Connolly had learned his lesson and had established the Citizen's Army as a means of protecting the workers. He was a very aggressive and somewhat impatient individual who had threatened to lead a rising by himself. Because activity by the small Citizen Army acting on its own would have elicited a swift and barbaric response from the British (also probably provoking the arrests of most of the Republican leadership), Pearse and Clarke had decided that Connolly had to be brought into the planning so that his efforts would not sabotage the plans of the IRB. Make no mistake, however, during the actual Rising, James Connolly was the man who provided the military leadership and the emotional stability which sustained the ordeal.

As they were fully aware of the consequences of their actions (except for the use of artillery by the British upon the city center of Dublin-Connolly's opinion prior to the Rising was that the British, as capitalists, could never destroy what capital had created), what of their mortality? As good Catholics, were they committing the gravest of sin in this doomed effort, was it essentially suicide? To the Republicans, the Rising was not a rebellion by anarchists and criminals bent upon destruction and/or looting. Because Pearse and Connolly had presented the

Proclamation of the Republic on the steps of the GPO that Monday at 1:00PM, and because copies of the Proclamation had been posted around the city, they had become a new nation, with a President (Pearse) and with its own armed forces. It was for that reason that after the Rising, public opinion turned in favor of the Republicans. The harshness of the executions and the treatment of those who had surrendered as mere criminals, led to calls from the public that the incarcerated Republicans be granted status as combatants. Therefore, the Rising had created a new Republic and as such, those who died during, or as a result of that battle, were soldiers of the Republic. There was no philosophical dilemma. Even hours prior to their individual executions, the leaders demonstrated a pure spirituality as evidenced by the writings of the Capuchin Friars who ministered them at Kilmainham. The stage had been set for the 'Six Days which shook an empire'.

There seems to be a restrained shyness about the Easter Rising, both in Ireland and among the emigrated Irish elsewhere. I have encountered this even in Canada. One must be very careful when approaching the subject with the Irish. If one asks about the event and tactlessly refers to it as a 'rebellion' a response will either not be forthcoming, or if one is received, it will be a real hesitance to discuss the matter.

The stated goals of the leaders of the Easter Rising was a fully free and independent island nation. As the treaty with Britain ending the Anglo-Irish War in 1921 partitioned the island, Irish nationalists feel as though the motivation of the Easter Rising have never been fulfilled, and further, that the 1921 treaty which plunged the Irish into the 1922 Civil War, not only left many in Ireland with emotional scars, but has been the impetus for *Sinn Fein* and the Irish Republican Army to the present day. For that reason, to show interest in the Easter Rising or to somehow glorify its participants would rankle those who descended from the 'anti-treaty' side of 1921.

As an American, it is my view that the Easter Rising is a fact of history. Taken in its historical context, it was a short event lasting from April 24th and lasting through May 12th, 1916 (the date of the last executions). It sparked the ideal that Ireland could be free (in whatever form) from external control and it energized Michael Collins and Arthur Griffith to lead that concept forward. The people of Ireland and those Irish abroad can maintain whatever feelings they may harbor about the Easter Rising, but they cannot erase the fact that it occurred. We in America had our own Civil War, not many years prior to the Easter Rising and it took perhaps four generations to ease the emotions for it. During those decades, however, historians preserved the record of the conflict, sites of battle were preserved and perpetuated into tourist attractions, movies were made and participants glorified. The old wounds were not erased, but allowed to ease with each passing generation. Hopefully, that will occur in Ireland once the six counties are reunited with the rest. That will happen, time is the only hindrance.

In the meantime, the government of the Republic of Ireland should insure that its citizens in particular and tourists in general have easy access to the historical sites. I have visited Beal na mBlath and it took me considerable time to find the town and then the memorial site. In my mind, that would be like going to Dallas and being unable to locate the Book Depository and the site of the John F. Kennedy assassination. I have also encountered problems finding Arbour Hill Cemetery, and the remains of Jacob's Biscuit Factory, the South Dublin Union, Richmond Barracks and the Mendicity Institution. These places are of critical historic importance in the founding of the Republic of Ireland.

It was a great pleasure to note that the celebrations in Dublin, sanctioned by the government and held over this past Easter weekend noting the 90th Anniversary of the Easter Rising were reported to have been peaceful as well as meaningful. This casts a positive tone for the run-up to the Centenary in 2016. We can only hope that the devolution agreement begun at St. Andrew's in 2006 and implemented in March, 2007, finally and forever extinguish the violence and death in Northern Ireland. As the 'Celtic Tiger' overflows to the North, it would seem that one benefit of prosperity would be to lessen sectarian tensions. Being Catholic or Protestant should become less important than being Irish.

TIMELINES: The Road to Irish Freedom from British Rule

Rebellions

1798 Rebellion which resulted in the ACT OF UNION which placed Ireland in the United Kingdom; 30,000 lives lost.

1803 Robert Emmet led this short-lived rebellion, crushed by the British.

1848 The Young Ireland Rebellion- another failure.

1867 The Fenian Uprising- crushed by British forces.

1916 Easter Rising: Six day event which presaged the Anglo-Irish War (The War for Independence) and the Free State.

Easter Rising

1858	Formation of the Irish Republican Brotherhood (IRB) or the Fenians.
1886	First Home Rule bill fails to pass.
1912	Third Home Rule bill passes.
1913	Irish Volunteers founded by Eoin MacNeill.
1914	World War I begins. Home Rule approved by both Houses of Parliament. Implementation tabled for duration of war.
1915	Sir Roger Casement arranges for arms shipment from Germany.
1916	January Plan for Easter Rising approved by the Military Council. April 21 German arms shipment discovered by the British. April 22 MacNeill cancels mobilization order for the Volunteers April 23 Military Council reschedules Rising for the following day. April 24 Easter Rising begins at noon.

The Road to the Republic

1916	April	The Easter Rising
	May	Executions of the leaders of the Rising
	August	Sir Roger Casement hanged in London
1918	December	Sinn Fein sweeps election in Ireland
1919	January	Establishment of the Dail by Sinn Fein
		The War for Independence begins
1920	December	Ireland partitioned
1921	July	Truce in the War for Independence
	December	Anglo-Irish Treaty established the Irish Free State
1922	June	Irish Civil War begins over treaty provisions
	August	Deaths of Arthur Griffith and Michael Collins
	December	Formal establishment of the Irish Free State
1923	April	Irish Civil War ends
1949	June	Irish Free State becomes the Republic of Ireland, six northern counties remain part of the United Kingdom

Republican Force Dispositions

Headquarters Battalion
General Post Office- Sackville Street
T. Clarke, P. Pearse, J Connolly, J Plunkett, S McDermott, The O'Rahilly

Fourth Battalion: South Dublin Union
James Street-Grand Canal
Eamonn Ceannt-Commandant
Cathal Brugha

First Battalion: Four Courts
Liffey River-North Brunswick St.
Ned Daly- Commandant
Sean Heuston: Mendicity Institute

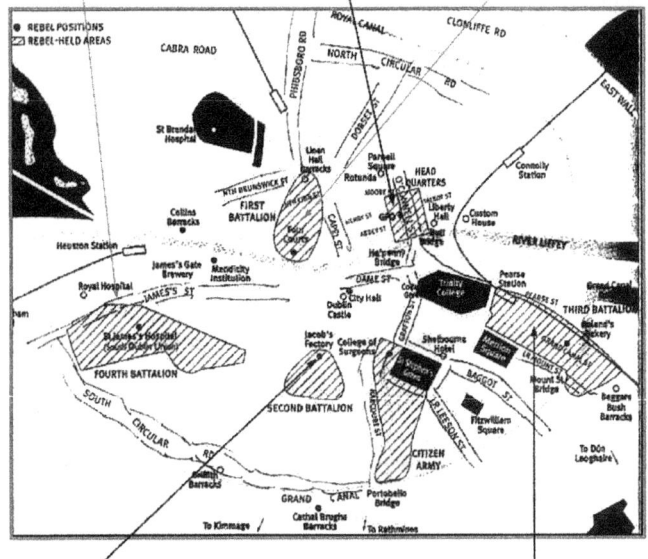

Second Battalion: Jacob's Biscuit Factory
Bride Street/Bishop Street
Thomas McDonough-Commandant
John McBride, Michael O'Hanrahan, Con Colbert

Third Battalion: Boland's Mills
Mount Street Lower/Grand Canal
Eamonn deValera- Commandant
Joseph O'Connor

Citizen Army: St. Stephen's Green
Royal College of Surgeons
Michael Mallin- Commandant
Countess Marlievicz

Forifications of the Rebels

EASTER RISING 1916 TIMELINE

	MONDAY April 24	TUESDAY April 25	WEDNESDAY April 26	THURSDAY April 27	FRIDAY April 28	SATURDAY April 29
MORNING	Volunteers & Citizen Army gather at Liberty Hall. They march to various pre-designated sites around the city. GPO seized at Noon. Dublin Castle attacked, lightly held but assault not pressed. Castle could have been captured. Magazine Fort in Phoenix Park assaulted, but not destroyed. City Hall captured.	British occupy Shelbourne Hotel. Attack begins on St. Stephen's Green- Citizen Army forced to occupy Royal College of Surgeons	Helga begins shelling Liberty Hall and Sackville Street	British continue shelling Sackville Street. James Connolly wounded in Middle Abbey Street	British continue shelling Sackville Street. Door-to-door fighting on North King Street, Church Street and Red Cow Lane	Fighting ends on North King Street
AFTERNOON	At 1:00PM, Patrick Pearse reads the Proclamation of the Republic. GPO fortified. St. Stephen's Green seized. Jacob's Factory seized. Boland's Mills seized. Four Courts seized and fortified. South Dublin Union seized. Mendicity Institution captured. Sean Heuston told to hold it for four hours.	Attack begins on 4th Battalion positions at South Dublin Union	Mendicity Institution evacuated and surrendered to British. Helga begins shelling Boland's positions. Mount Street Bridge 200 British killed by evening. Artillery attack begins on GPO	Heavy British assault upon South Dublin Union - 4th battalion holds. Heroic stand by Cathal Brugha.	Roof of GPO on fire. The O'Rahilly killed in Moore Street. Headquarters Batt evacuates GPO - moves down Moore St.	Flag of surrender presented to British by Elizabeth O'Farrell. Patrick Pearse surrenders to British General Lowe. All other garrisons surrender.
EVENING	City Hall retaken by British					Prisoners held overnight outside at Rotunda Hospital
CODE:	Headquarters Battalion GPO Pearse-Connolly-Clarke	1st Battalion Four Courts Ned Daly	2nd Battalion Jacob's Biscuit Factory Thomas MacDonagh	3rd Battalion Boland's Mills Eamonn deValera	4th Battalion South Dublin Union Eamonn Ceannt	Citizen Army St. Stephen's Green Michael Mallin

copyright - Old Kilmainham Ltd., 2006

ORGANIZATIONS

CITIZEN ARMY

The Citizen Army was founded in 1913 as a means of protecting workers who publicly expressed grievances. During the famous lockout of that year, the workers were both harassed and attacked by the military and the police. The group was established and led by James Connolly who directed the organization from Liberty Hall, headquarters of the Irish Transportation and General Workers Union (ITGWU) located on Beresford Place. That group was one of the first in Ireland to offer quality for both men and women.

At the outset of the Easter Rising, the Citizen Army mustered about 220 of its small force of 250. The group's main responsibility was the seizure and security of St. Stephen's Green. Immediately, however, that proved tenuous and Commandant Mallin was forced to retire to the Royal College of Surgeons, located on the west end of St. Stephen's Green. The banner for the Citizen Army was the Plough and Stars colored in both green and yellow.

IRISH REPUBLICAN BROTHERHOOD (IRB)

This is the main group which traditionally advocated armed revolt as a means of achieving independence for Ireland from Britain. It was aimed at people of Irish descent from around the world as well as the people of Ireland. It was originally founded by James Stephen's in the 1850's. During the 1867 Revolt, the IRB co-operated with the Irish Parliamentary Party of Parnell, although the latter was dedicated to non-violence. The 1867 Revolt was a disaster.

The IRB had a very strong branch in America which was called the Fenian Brotherhood, a name which was later changed to *Clan na Gael* and directed by John Devoy.

During the 1880's and 1890's, the British Special Irish Branch nearly destroyed the organization. It was revitalized around 1910 by Thomas Clarke and Sean McDermott. Later, Patrick Pearse was brought into the group and the IRB was able to infiltrate the Irish Volunteers and make that organization the military arm of the Republican movement. On the eve of the Easter Rising, the IRB had a membership in excess of 2000.

CUMANN na mBAN

This group was the women's league which acted as an auxiliary to the Irish Volunteers and was founded by Countess Markievicz, Agnes O'Farrell, Jennie Wyse-Power and Louise Gavan Duffy in 1913. The group was very nationalistic and trained in first aid and the maintenance and use of weapons. During the Rising, the Cumann na mBan did most of the domestic chores for the fighters (cooking and first aid), but also involved itself more fully by being couriers and participating in combat.

FIANNA EIREANN

This was a youth organization founded in 1913 by Countess Markievicz and Bulmer Hobson for the purpose of the installation of nationalistic principles and the promotion of the Irish culture and language. It included both boys and girls and was active during the Easter Rising, particularly at the Mendicity Institution.

IRISH VOLUNTEERS

Organization which was founded in 1913 and its purpose was as a counter to the Ulster Volunteers. The latter group was formed in Northern Ireland as a military force to face any threat from Republicans or Nationalists. The aim of the Volunteers was to gain and protect the rights of all the people of Ireland. Eventually the Volunteers would claim 100,000 members. By 1915, the Volunteers were headed by Eoin MacNeill. He, along with Bulmer Hobson and The O'Rahilly, formed the less-militant part of the leadership while Patrick Pearse, Thomas Clarke and Thomas MacDonagh were the hawks in opposition. By the time of the Easter Rising, the Volunteers had been infiltrated by the IRB and were being pushed towards violence.

MILITARY COUNCIL OF THE IRB

In 1915, Patrick Pearse, Joseph Plunkett, Sean McDermott, Eamonn Ceannt and Thomas Clarke formed the Military Council. This group effectively took control of the Irish Republican Brotherhood and secretly planned the Easter Rising. The planning was accomplished without the knowledge of the Supreme Council or the IRB or the leader of the Irish Volunteers, Eoin MacNeill.

By early 1916, James Connolly was brought into the Military Council as a means of controlling his aggressive stance towards an uprising, and also to gain the use of Connolly's small military organization, the Citizen Army. By March, 1916, the seventh member of the Military Council of the IRB, Thomas MacDonagh was in place. The Military Council of the IRB planned, organized and led the Easter Rising.

SINN FEIN

Arthur Griffith formed Sinn Fein in 1905. The literal translation means "ourselves", not the common misconception "ourselves alone". The party was formed to perpetuate the concept of a dual monarchy, which envisioned both an Irish and British King in control of Ireland. Regardless of the initial purpose of Sinn Fein, it was/is an aggressive nationalist political entity. Griffith,, who was a newspaperman, used the term Sinn Fein as the title of one of his newspapers.

In 1915, Sinn Fein, as a political movement had nearly ceased to exist. By a stroke of good fortune, however, the British mistakenly attributed the Easter Rising to Sinn Fein, dubbing the event the 'Sinn Fein Rebellion'.

IRISH REPUBLICAN ARMY (IRA)

The IRA is a military organization which descended from the Irish Volunteers of the Easter Rising. It was christened by the Dail Eireann in 1919 as the legitimate military organization of the UDI Irish Republic, the Irish state proclaimed by Patrick Pearse in 1916.

At a Sinn Fein convention in Dublin on October, 27, 1917, it was decided to reorganize the Irish Volunteers. At that time, nationalist Ireland was recovering from the losses of the Easter Rising and was also preparing a platform for the eventual peace conference which would end World War I. Prominent personalities were participants at that convention and the result was that Eamonn deValera was elected President of Sinn Fein.

Personalities of the Easter Rising

Thomas Clarke
(March 11, 1857- May 3, 1916)

Thomas Clarke was born on the Isle of Wight to Irish parents. The family eventually settled in County Tyrone. He emigrated early on to America and found work as an explosives tradesman in New York City.

Tom joined the I.R.B. and was sent to London on a mission to destroy a target with explosives. He was captured before completing his task and forced to serve fifteen years in Pentonville Prison. During his prison years, he nearly went mad, but was able to maintain his sanity through his stubborn determination for Irish nationalism and eventual freedom.

After release, he married Ned Daly's sister, Kathleen. After another period of time in America, he and his family returned to Dublin, arriving in 1907. He opened a tobacco shop at 75 Parnell Street which became a meeting place for I.R.B. activities. It was here that he and Sean MacDermott began the plan for the Easter Rising.

As he was the oldest and most respected member of the Military Council of the I.R.B., he was given the honor of being the first to sign the Proclamation of the Republic of Ireland. He was also among the first group to be executed at Kilhaimham on May 3, 1916. All of those executed at Kilmainham were buried in quick-lime in the back yard of Arbour Hill Prison, so that their remains could not be martyred.

At the time of his capture from the GPO, and unknown to him, his wife was pregnant. She subsequently suffered a miscarriage. She never remarried, but remained very active in Republican affairs.

James Connolly
(June 5, 1868- May 12, 1916)

James Connolly was born in Scotland of Irish parents. He began working at a very young age in the printing industry. At the age of fourteen, he joined the British Army, where he was subsequently stationed in Ireland for seven years.

Connolly returned to Scotland where he became a committed Marxist. Shortly, thereafter, he moved to Dublin where he took a position as an organizer for the Socialist Society, founding the Irish Socialist Party and its newspaper, *The Worker's Republic*.

Later on, after a trip to America, Connolly began working for Jim Larkin and his new union, the ITGWU. Through this connection and because of the Lockout of 1913, Connolly founded the Irish Citizen Army.

The Citizen Army, although small, was highly organized and personally trained by James Connolly. It was his view that concurrent with protecting the ITGWU personnel, that the unit would lead an uprising against Britain once the Great War had begun. He was so aggressive in his insistence upon armed conflict with Britain, that he was co-opted by the Military Council of the IRB into that organization to forestall any preemptive action by the Citizen Army.

During the Easter Rising, Connolly was Commander-General of the Dublin Brigade. Essentially, more than anyone, he was the military brains and man-of-action during the six days. He maintained his position despite having been wounded twice, the second which quickly turned to gangrene. In fact, he was so badly wounded that he could not stand to be executed, but was in fact shot while strapped to a chair on May 12th at Kilmainham.

Thomas MacDonagh
(February 1, 1878- May 3, 1916)

Thomas MacDonagh was born in County Tipperary and followed his parents into the teaching profession. He was educated at Rockwell College and University College Dublin. His interest in the Irish Language led him to join the Gaelic League in 1901. While in the Aran Islands studying Gaelic, he met Patrick Pearse.

He assisted Pearse in the founding of St. Enda's School in Rathfarnham, Dublin in 1908. In 1913, he became a university lecturer.

MacDonagh was a founding member of the Irish Volunteers in 1913 and became a member of the I.R.B. in 1915. Immediately preceding the Easter Rising, he was brought onto the Military Council.

Thomas MacDonagh spent the Easter Rising as Commander of the battalion at Jacob's Biscuit Factory. He was a signatory of the Proclamation and was executed at Kilmainham on May 3rd.

Patrick Pearse
(November 10, 1879- May 3, 1916)

Patrick Pearse was born of Anglo-Irish parents, his father having been an English carver. Pearse was educated at the Christian Brother's School in Dublin and at the Royal University. He was also an attorney, but he did not practice law.

His interest in the Irish Language led him to join the Gaelic League and he became editor of its newspaper. Pearse was an early supporter of Home Rule, but eventually became convinced that only physical force could lead to independence.

Pearse was recruited into the I.R.B. in 1912 and later became a member of its Military Council. It was his idea to deceive Eoin MacNeill (leader of the Irish Volunteers) and wrest effective control of the Volunteers for military action against the British.

By Easter 1916, Pearse had been elected head of the Provisional Government of the Republic of Ireland and he delivered the Proclamation of independence from the front steps of the GPO on Easter Monday, 1916.

As head of the government, Pearse delivered all of the important directives during the week of the Easter Rising. He ordered the evacuation of the wounded and most of the women from the GPO, he made every effort to insure that he was the last to leave the ravaged building, and he personally surrendered his forces to the British.

Patrick Pearse faced court martial at Richmond Barracks and being found guilty, was sentenced to death by firing squad. That order was carried out at Kilmainham on May 3rd.

Eamonn Ceannt

(September 21, 1881- May 8, 1916)

Eamonn Ceannt was born in County Galway. His father had been an R.I.C. (Royal Irish Constabulary). Growing up, he became proficient as an uileann piper and was employed as a clerk for the Dublin Corporation.

Ceannt joined the Gaelic League in 1900, and was a founding member of the Irish Volunteers. In 1913, he joined the I.R.B. and eventually becoming a member of both the Supreme Council and the Military Council. He was also a signatory of the Proclamation of the Irish Republic.

Eamonn Ceannt was Commander of the Fourth Battalion which took control of the South Dublin Union as well as Marrowbone Lane and the Rialto Bridge area. His second-in-command was Cathal Brugha. The Fourth Battalion surrendered at the end of the Rising and Ceannt was executed at Kilmainham on May 8th.

Sean McDermott
(February 28, 1883- May 12, 1916)

Sean McDermott was born in County Leitrim. As a youth, he had worked as a tram conductor in Belfast. It was there that he was sworn into the I.R.B. By 1908, he had been transferred to Dublin and became a close friend and confidant of Thomas Clarke.

From that time forward, McDermott devoted all of his energies to the I.R.B. and became its best known personality due to his recruitment travels throughout Ireland. In 1913, he was a founding member of the Irish Volunteers. He became secretary of the Supreme Council and of the Military Council. He was a signatory of the Proclamation and a member of the Provisional Government.

During the Rising, McDermott remained at the GPO and was continuously an inspiration to the garrison. It was McDermott who was the strength behind the final surrender. He was executed at Kilmainham on May 12th.

Joseph Mary Plunkett
(November 21, 1887- May 4, 1916)

Joseph Plunkett was a keen scholar and the son of a papal count who was born in Dublin. He had very close ties with literary Dublin and was editor of the *Irish Review*.

Plunkett joined both the I.R.B. and the Volunteers. He ventured to Germany in 1914 in hopes of achieving German assistance for Irish independence. His family's estate in Kimmage was used as a training base for the Volunteers.

Plunkett suffered from ill health and had had an operation for glandular tuberculosis only days before the Easter Rising. He also had to postpone his wedding as it conflicted with the Rising.

He struggled out of his sick bed to take part and was assisted by his Aide de Camp, Michael Collins, during the Rising. As a member of the Military Council of the I.R.B., he had a great deal of influence in the decision process from the GPO. He was also a signatory of the Proclamation of the Republic.

Just hours before his execution, he was allowed to marry his sweetheart, Grace Gifford, in the chapel at Kilmainham. Three hours later, he was executed on May 4th.

Cornelius (Con) Colbert
(1888- May 8, 1916)

Con Colbert was born in Athea, County Limerick in 1888 and was educated at the Christian Brother's School at North Richmond Street after his parents had moved to Dublin.

In 1913, he joined the Volunteers and became one of its first drill instructors. He was quickly appointed Captain of F Company, Fourth Battalion, a position he held throughout the Easter Rising.

In the years before 1916, Colbert devoted his time to organizing and training boys and men who would participate in the historic event. His wages were meager, but he spent almost every penny on the advancement of the movement. Patrick Pearse asked him to become a drill instructor at St. Enda's School and he agreed. He was offended when Pearse offered to pay him for his services.

Colbert served under Eamonn Ceannt at South Dublin Union. Initially he was given command of Wadkin's Brewery and later the Jamison Distillery on Marrowbone Lane.

After the surrender, Colbert was tried at Richmond Barracks. At his court martial, Colbert's only comment was "I have nothing to say". After being led into Stonebreaker's Yard at Kilmainham for his execution, he recommended to the officer in charge of the firing squad that the target on his chest be moved closer to his heart.

Con Colbert was executed on May 8th.

John MacBride
(1865-May 5, 1916)

John MacBride was born in County Mayo. His education included studies in medicine. He was an early member of the I.R.B. and undertook a mission for it to the USA in 1896. Later he emigrated to South Africa.

While there, he organized the 1798 Centenary Celebration. During the Boer War, he joined the Irish Brigade, fighting against the British. After the British victory, he moved to Paris where he married Maud Gonne. The marriage was short-lived but resulted in a son, Sean (or Seagan) who would later become President of Ireland.

Although MacBride was a member of the Supreme Council of the I.R.B., he had no part in the planning of the Easter Rising. He served under Thomas MacDonagh at Jacob's Biscuit Factory and was executed at Kilmainham on May 5th.

Edward (Ned) Daly
(February 28, 1891- May 4, 1916)

Ned Daly was born in Limerick and lived in a house on Frederick Street. As both his father and uncle were Fenians, Daly had a strong Republican background. Later on, his sister Kathleen would marry Thomas Clarke, another leader of the Easter Rising.

Ned joined the Volunteers in 1913 and quickly became a company captain. Before the Rising, he had been promoted to battalion commander and was given the charge to hold the Four Courts area. Though tremendously outnumbered, Daly's command held out until the very end and inflicted heavy casualties upon the British.

A detachment from Daly's First Battalion under Sean Heuston made an extremely gallant and successful stand for three days at the Mendicity Institution on the South side of the Liffey. Also from his command, the heavy fighting in the Church/ North King Street area presented some of the most intense fighting during the Easter Rising.

After Patrick Pearse ordered the surrender of all the rebels, Daly surrendered his troops, marched them to Sackville Street, and went into captivity with the rest. He was court-martialed at Richmond Barracks and swiftly executed at Kilmainham on May 4th.

Sean Heuston
(February 21, 1897- May 8, 1916)

Not much is known of the early life of Sean Heuston, but at the outset of the Easter Rising, he was a member of Ned Daly's First Battalion. Daly gave the young Heuston the task of taking and holding the Mendicity Institution for "two hours" as a blocking action against British reinforcements while Daly established his defensive positions.

Heuston had at his disposal a few *Fianna Eireann* scouts between the ages of twelve and sixteen. The deployment took place at midday on April 24th. By Wednesday morning, two Volunteer dispatch runners had broken through very dangerous areas to deliver a message to James Connolly at the GPO from Sean Heuston. His message was that he needed immediate reinforcements as his force of twenty had been heavily engaged with several hundred British troops. Before aid could be sent, Heuston was forced to surrender. The British were angered and astounded by both the number and ages of the few defenders.

Sean Heuston was executed at Kilmainham on May 8th. The former Kingsbridge Railway station was renamed Heuston Station.

Michael O'Hanrahan
(March 17, 1877- May 4, 1916)

Michael O'Hanrahan was born in New Ross, Wexford. After moving to Carlow, O'Hanrahan was educated at the Christian Brother's Academy and Carlow College Academy. Upon completing his education, he went to Dublin and worked at the Clo Cumann printing works. He wrote two novels, one of which was published after his death.

His father had been a Fenian who had taken part in the 1867 Rising. As Republican fervor was in his blood, he joined the Volunteers in 1913 and was also active in the Gaelic League.

Later he became quartermaster of the Volunteers and a fulltime member of the headquarters staff. During the Easter Rising, he fought at Jacob's Biscuit Factory under Thomas MacDonagh. He was executed at Kilmainham on May 4th.

William Pearse
(November 15, 1881 - May 4, 1916)

Willie Pearse was the younger brother of Patrick Pearse, the President of the Provisional Government of the Irish Republic. Willie, however, was only a private in the Volunteers.

Willie adored his brother and followed him everywhere, including into the GPO on Easter Monday. His only crime seems to have been with relationship with Patrick Pearse. He was not involved in any decision-making regarding the Easter Rising and should have suffered the same fate as any other private i.e., perhaps internment and eventual release. Therefore, next to Francis Sheehy-Skeffington, Willie's death was the most inexplicable act of retribution by the British after the surrender.

Willie Pearse was executed at Kilmainham on May 4th.

Cathal Brugha

(July 18, 1874- July 6, 1922)

Irish nationalist and revolutionary, Cathal Brugha was initially a candle maker in Dublin. He was educated at Belvedere College and joined the Gaelic League in 1899 and the Volunteers in 1913.

During the Easter Rising, he was second-in-command to Eamonn Ceannt at the South Dublin Union. It was there that he displayed perhaps the greatest display of heroism during the entire week. Alone, he held off a determined British assault. Ceannt was certain the Brugha had died. As he prepared to retreat with the remaining Volunteers, Ceannt heard whispered singing coming from a nearby garden. After gaining enough courage to investigate, they found Cathal Brugha braced against a wall goading the British to charge his position.

His would were so life-threatening that the British did not bother to arrest him after the surrender; they fully expected him to die.

He managed to recover, however, and went on to become Minister of Defense during the War for Independence. After the treaty ending that war had been signed, Cathal Brugha took the anti-treaty side during the Civil War.

He was killed on O'Connell Street as he emerged from a fortified hotel. He had sent all of his colleagues out and refused numerous requests for surrender.

Michael Mallin
(birth: unknown- May 8, 1916)

Michael Mallin was a member of the Citizen Army under James Connolly. Bt trade, he was a silk weaver. Connolly entrusted Mallin with the only Citizen Army garrison during the Rising, St. Stephen's Green.

At the Green, with Countess Markievicz as his immediate subordinate, he set about immediately to clear the area of civilians, form barricades and entrench his troops. He made a grave tactical error by not taking the surrounding high rise buildings. From the outset, his garrison was devastated by withering fire and he moved his force to the Royal College of Surgeons at the west end of the Green.

After he and the Countess surrendered their command to the British, Mallin was court martialed and executed at Kilmainham on May 8th.

Eamonn deValera
(October 14, 1882- August 29, 1975)

Eamonn deValera was born in New York, but at the age of two he was sent to live with his grandmother in Burree, County Limerick. He later became a mathematics teacher (1904) and joined the Gaelic League in 1908. By 1913, he was a member of the Volunteers.

During the Easter Rising, deValera commanded the Third Battalion headquartered at Boland's Bakery. Men under his command inflicted the heaviest casualties upon the British during the heroic stand at Mount Street Bridge. The Third Battalion was the only Volunteer command which allowed no female participation; these were deValera's explicit instructions. Commander deValera surrendered his troops at the end of the Rising, was court martialed and sentenced to death. That penalty was commuted, however, due to his American citizenship. Thus he was the only commander to escape execution. He was sentenced to life imprisonment at Lincoln in England.

A very daring escape was planned and executed by Michael Collins which allowed deValera to return to Ireland and take a very active role in the struggle for independence. He was President of Sinn Fein (1917-1926), President of the First Dail (1919), and President of the Irish Republic (1921). He opposed the treaty and for against the Free State. In 1927, he established the *Fianna Fail* Party and by 1932, controlled the government. He was Taoiseach (1937- 1948, 1951- 1954, 1957- 1959) and President from 1959- 1973.

Countess Markievicz
(February 4, 1868- July 15, 1927)

Constance Gore-Booth, who became Countess Markievicz, was born at Lissadel, County Sligo, of a prominent Anglo- Irish family. Although raised in the finest circles of Nineteenth Century Ireland, she became in nationalist and social causes while in her twenties. She joined the *Inghinidhe ne hEireann* and the subsequent *Cumann na mBann*. The Countess was also a founding member of *Fianna Eireann*. During the 1913 Lockout, she served in the soup kitchens in support of the workers. It was at this time that she came into contact with James Connolly and the ITGWU. That organization was the first in Ireland to include women on an equal basis with men. She also joined the Citizen Army.

During the Easter Rising, Countess Marlievicz was second in command (to Michael Mallin) at St. Stephen's Green and the Royal College of Surgeons. After the surrender, the Countess faced court martial and was sentenced to death. Being a woman, the sentence was commuted, much against her wishes.

In 1918, she was elected to the House of Commons, but refused to take her seat. The Countess opposed the treaty. She joined the *Fianna Fail Party* and was elected to the Dail in 1927, but died later that year.

Michael O'Rahilly (The O'Rahilly)
(April 22, 1875- April 28, 1916)

Born in Ballylongford, County Kerry, O'Rahilly was educated at Royal University of Ireland in Dublin. In 1898, he left for America to make his way in the world. After his marriage to Nancy Brown, he remained in America until 1902, when he returned to Ireland.

He became very interested in Irish History and thoroughly researched his family genealogy, publishing his findings in 1910. He assumed the ancient Irish tradition of referring to himself as "The O'Rahilly" i.e., the oldest living male of the family.

The O'Rahilly wrote for various nationalistic publications including *United Irishman, Sinn Fein,* and *Irish Freedom.* He was co-founder of the Irish Volunteers in 1913. After the split in that organization in 1914, The O'Rahilly remained with the smaller Volunteers under Eoin MacNeill.

As MacNeill attempted to stop the Easter Rising, it was The O'Rahilly who drove throughout Southern Ireland carrying the stand-down order from Dublin. Upon returning to Dublin on Monday, April 24th, he quickly realized that the Rising was going forward anyway. He reported to the GPO and said "Because I helped wind the clock, I came to hear it strike".

He fought gallantly at the GPO and led a party out of the building just prior to evacuation. While doing so, he was killed, becoming the only rebel leader to die in battle during the Easter Rising

Sir Roger Casement
(September 1, 1864- August 3, 1916)

Roger Casement began his career in the British Colonial service. He was eventually knighted in 1911 for exposing brutality and exploitation in colonies. After retiring from the civil service, Sir Roger returned to Ireland where he joined the Irish Volunteers in 1913.

It was his idea to travel to Germany during World War I and form the Irish Brigade from German prisoners, and that the brigade would eventually fight for Irish freedom during the Rising. The brigade never materialized, and Casement returned to Ireland aboard a submarine at the same time as the arms shipment from Germany was scheduled to arrive. The arms landing was a failure and Casement was captured. He had hoped to stop the Rising. He was tried for treason and convicted. He was hanged at Pentonville Prison on August 3, 1916. In 1965, his remains were returned to Ireland where he was given a state funeral at Glasnevin Cemetery.

Francis Sheehy-Skeffington
(1878- April 25, 1916)

Skeff, as he was known, was born in County Cavan in 1878. He attended University College and became a lifelong pacifist and feminist. Eventually, he became a writer and focused upon peace, equality and nationalism. In 1905, he joined the United Irish League.

He had ties to labor and was named vice-chairman of the Citizen Army, a role he would assume on the condition that the C.A. would only act in a defensive posture. He was a friend of many of the key figures in the I.R.B. and worked tirelessly to convince them that the road to freedom did not include guns, but rather intellect.

His only role in the Easter Rising was that of a neutral. While on the streets, he was arrested by the British, and as a witness to a murder, he was executed. He quickly became an innocent martyr.

Sir John Maxwell
Military Commander, British Forces

General Maxwell had returned to England from the Middle East in March, 1916, and was sent to Ireland to take command from General Friend. His mandate was to quell the Rising and restore order.

His immediate task was to cordon areas of the city into which the Republicans had established themselves. The area of primary concern was Sackville Street and the GPO.

Contrary to the beliefs of James Connolly, the British in general, and General Maxwell in particular, were fully prepared to use artillery in smashing the enemy positions. The result of that strategy was that most of Sackville Street was destroyed. The effect was that Patrick Pearse was forced to seek surrender terms for his force after vacating the GPO.

General Maxwell accepted uncondional surrender from Pearse. He had all of the leaders tried under court martial. They were found guilty of treason and all given death sentences (two were reprived). Within a matter of two weeks, Maxwell had destroyed the center of Dublin, tried the leaders of the Rising and had them all executed. His swift justice provided and equally swift change in sentiment among the Irish people towards the Rising and the martyred leaders.

Dr. Kathleen Lynn

Kathleen Lynn received her medical degree in 1899, and as such, was the first woman resident practicing medicine in Dublin. She was made Chief Medical Officer of the Citizen Army by James Connolly.

Her posting during the Easter Rising was to the small City Hall garrison. When the commanding officer was shot, she as second in rank, assumed command. She continued to serve the Republican cause throughout her life and practiced medicine well into her eighties.

Winifred Carney

Winifred Carney was secretary to James Connolly and his labor organization. She had also been trained in the Citizen Army and was a crack shot. On Easter Monday, she took her place next to Connolly and marched off to the GPO.

She remained there for the entire week, enduring the fighting, fire, and worst of all, the wounds to James Connolly. When Pearse ordered the women to leave the GPO on Thursday, three absolutely refused including Carney.

She helped carry Connolly's wounded body through the holes in the walls, moving in that manner from building to building. She stayed with him, until the surrender.

Grace Gifford Plunkett

Truly the most sentimentally tragic female figure of the Easter Rising was Grace Gifford. A double wedding had been planned with Grace to marry Joseph Plunkett and Plunkett's sister Geraldine to marry Thomas Dillon.

Because Joseph was a member of the Military Council, and because of the date of the planned Rising, the wedding had to be postponed. Subsequently, they did marry, but it was in Kilmainham gaol just three hours before Joseph was executed. Because of that, she is, of course, the inspiration for the song, "Grace".

After the Easter Rising and for the remainder of her life, Grace Gifford Plunkett never remarried.

Elizabeth O'Farrell

A nurse by trade, Elizabeth O'Farrell had been involved in feminist women's organizations prior to the Easter Rising. Her place in Irish history was assured by her heroics during that event.

When MacNeill sent out the order on Easter Sunday cancelling the Volunteers' maneuvers for the following day, Patrick Pearse used O'Farrell as a courier with the counter-mandering order. She spent Easter Sunday evening and the next morning completing her mission before returning to the GPO.

During Easter week, she remained inside the GPO administering aid to the wounded. When Pearse ordered all of the women to leave, O'Farrell, Julia Grenan and Winifred Carney refused. When it came time to surrender, Elizabeth O'Farrell risked her life for two days carrying the surrender document. The famous photograph of Pearse surrendering to General Lowe does not easily show O'Farrell standing on Pearse's right.

Synopsis: The Easter Rising

EVENTS IMMEDIATELY PRIOR TO EASTER MONDAY

The leadership of the Irish Republican Brotherhood had infiltrated the Irish Volunteers of Eoin MacNeill and had secretly planned a nationwide rising for Easter Sunday, 1916. Critical to the scheme was the receipt of arms and ammunition from Germany which were to be landed in Tralee before the planned rising. The arms did arrive at the appointed time aboard the *Aud*, but the Volunteers were confused about the day of the landing and therefore missed their opportunity. The British captured the ship, but the cargo was lost when the ship was scuttled just outside Queenstown (Cork) harbor. Because the munitions failed to appear, MacNeill informed Patrick Pearse that he would not support the planned rising, but would in fact order the Volunteers to stand down. Those two events doomed any chance there may have been for success.

Late in the afternoon, Easter Sunday, the Military Council of the IRB decided that the rising would occur the following day at noon. There was little hesitation in their decision despite the setbacks. Pearse, James Connolly and Thomas Clarke were well aware that their efforts were doomed to failure, but they were convinced that time was running out and if the decision were not made, most of the leadership would be arrested and jailed. That scenario would have totally crippled the nationalist movement.

MONDAY, APRIL 24

As Easter Monday was a Bank Holiday, Dublin's population had decreased considerably as many people had left the city for the seaside or the horse races at Fairyhouse. It was an unusually sunny Spring day when the rebels began to assemble at Libery Hall around 11:00AM. Between the Citizen Army and the Volunteers, only about 1200 men mustered. That was considerably less than originally anticipated due mainly to MacNeill's cancellation order published in the newspaper the previous day. Despite the numbers, units were dispatched to designated sites, albeit with greatly reduced capabilities.

The initial plan called for the seizure of key locations: the GPO, Four Courts, Boland's Mils, St. Stephen's Green and other tactical locations primarily selected to disrupt British lines of communication. These sites included the South Dublin Union, the Mendicity Institution, Mount Street Bridge, Jacob's Biscuit Factory as well as Dublin City Hall. All of the objectives were achieved within a short period of time. In fact, the Cork Hill Gate of Dublin Castle witnessed the first shots of the Rising, and had the attack been pressed forward, the seat of British authority in Ireland, the Castle, could probably have been secured easily. As it was, the rebels at the gate were afraid that the Castle was heavily defended and did not perpetuate their advantage. That group of rebels satisfied themselves with holding the City Hall.

Headquarters for the Easter Rising was established in the General Post Office (GPO) on Sackville Street. Here, James Connolly assumed military control. The building was immediately heavily barricaded as were the surrounding streets. At around 1:00PM, Patrick Pearse, Head of the Provisional Government of the Republic of Ireland, along with James Connolly and Thomas Clarke, emerged from the GPO and read the Proclamation of the Republic. National flags were raised over the GPO, one the Irish tricolor and the other the Plough & Stars of the Citizen Army.

In the GPO area during the afternoon, the DMP (Dublin Metropolitan Police) were withdrawn as they were ill-equipped to deal with a military confrontation. As a consequence of no police presence, large scale looting commenced all along Sackville Street. At around 3:30PM, a troop of British cavalry (Lancers) began a charge down the street from the Parnell Monument. They were easy prey for the rebels and several lancers were either killed or wounded, while the remainder retreated back up Sackville Street. The rest of the day at the GPO was spent in continuous fortification of the building and taking other buildings along the street.

At St. Stephen's Green, the Citizen Army Brigade under Commandant Mallin and his second-in-command, Countess Markievicz, ordered all civilians to leave the park. They barricaded the gates and the outlying streets. The rebels in the Green were ordered to dig trenches for cover; sadly, the surrounding tall buildings (particularly the Shelbourne Hotel) were not taken and these soon rendered occupation of St. Stephen's Green useless. Fortunately for Mallin, his force did wrest control of the Royal College of Surgeons on the western end of the Green.

Commandant Ceannt established the Fourth Battalion successfully inside the South Dublin Union facilities. However, the sheer expanse of the site made it impossible to fortify properly. Ceannt sent detachments to prearranged sites at the Jameson Distillery on Marrowbone Lane and Watkin's Brewery on Ardee Street.

Meanwhile, Commandant deValera established control in the Boland's Mills area. The primary objective for this Third Battalion was to prevent British reinforcements from entering the city after disembarkation at the

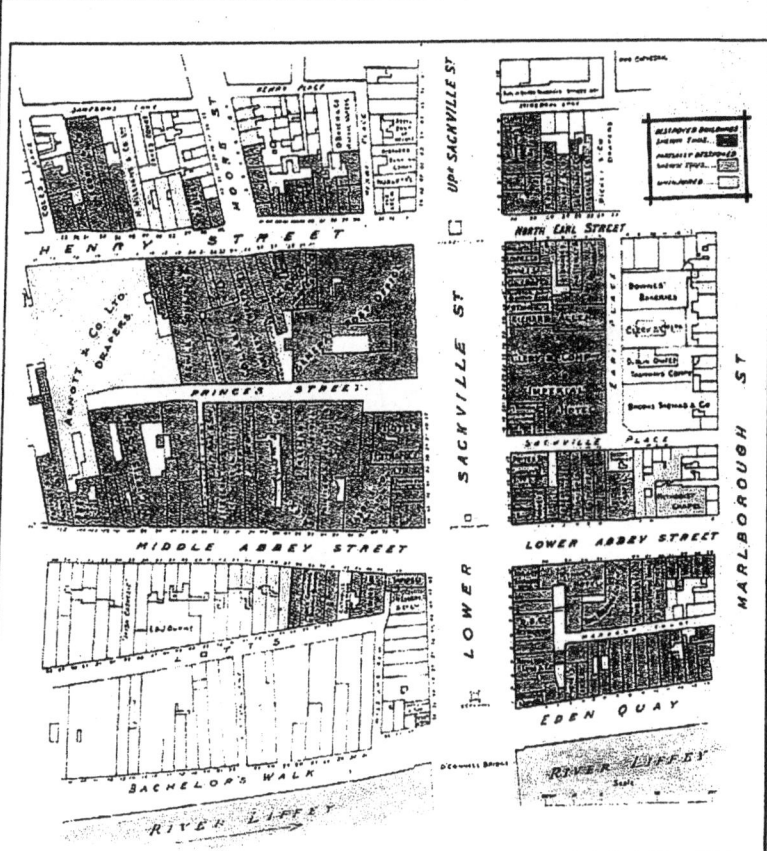

The General Post Office area as shown on a map issued by the Hibernian Fire and General Insurance Company shortly after the Rising. (O'Mahony Collection).

The GPO Area

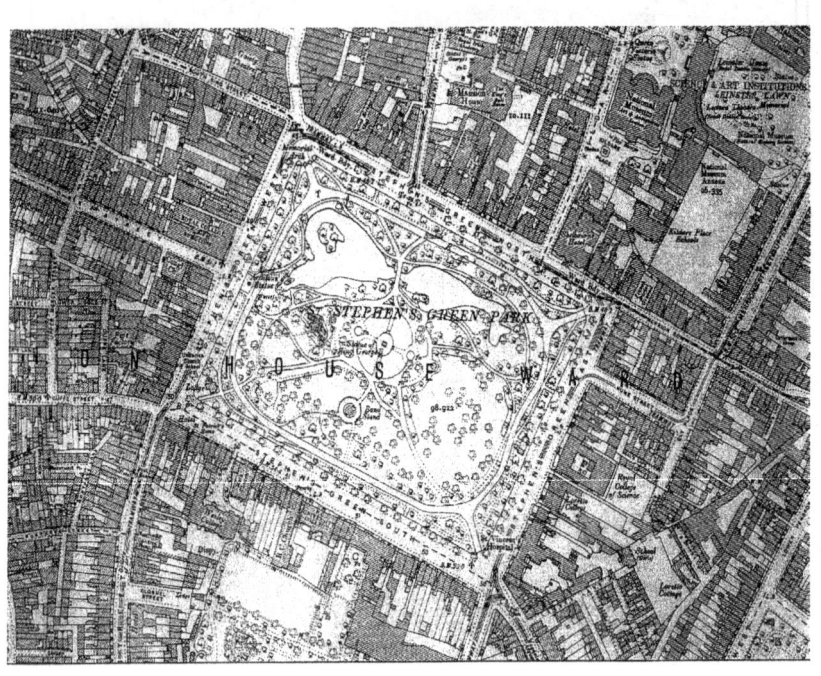

St. Stephen's Green

main seaport of Kingstown. Initially, deValera was to deploy his forces all the way from Kingstown into Dublin as far as the Westland Row Railway Station. Owing to the fact that very few of his men reported for duty, deValera could only occupy his positions very lightly, and no further south than the junction of Pembroke and Northumberland Roads. In essence, the Third Battalion would have to await and withstand the British assault rather than pre-empt it. Critical sites occupied in this area were: Clanwilliam House, No. 25 Northumberland Road and the railway line from Kingstown.

Commandant MacDonagh took his Second Battalion to the Bride Street area and occupied the massive Jacob's Biscuit Factory. That structure possessed two very tall towers which afforded the rebels excellent fields of fire in all directions- North to Dublin Castle, East to St. Stephen's Green and South to Portobello Barracks. The factory itself was impregnable to infantry assault and the surrounding area was composed of very narrow streets and alleys.

The remaining battalion, the First, under Commandant Daly occupied the Four Courts located on the Quays along the Liffey, along with Church Street, North King Street and the Mendicity Institution across the Liffey. The latter was under the command of nineteen year old Sean Heuston and a few *Fianna Eireann* scouts. The task there was to hold the position for a couple of hours while the remainder of the First Battalion established barricades and occupied adjacent positions.

The occupation of City Hall by a detachment of the Citizen Army was beaten back by the British toward late Monday afternoon, giving the rebels their only setback of the day.

By nightfall, the Republicans held all of their positions except City Hall. Everything had been accomplished despite their low numbers, but assisted by the fact that Easter Monday was a holiday. The British had been completely surprised. James Connolly remarked to those inside the GPO that having lasted a day meant that the British had been defeated. Pearse commented that their rising had lasted longer than the two previous under Wolfe Tone and Robert Emmet.

TUESDAY APRIL 25

Early Tuesday morning, the British had begun to mobilize their forces in Ireland to deal with the Rising. General Lowe had no idea how many rebels had mobilized, nor was he aware of their exact deployment. His plan involved the establishment of a cordon around the rebel strong points to sever their lines of communications and when properly reinforced, he planned to eliminate their positions.

Toward that end, by Tuesday morning, there were about 5000 British troops on their way to Dublin. Also in the morning, General Lowe had dispatched about one hundred troops to the Shelbourne Hotel to deal with the rebels in St. Stephen's Green. By noon, with the loss of City Hall the previous evening, the British were able to establish a line of control from Kingsbridge Station to Trinity College, effectively isolating the command center at the GPO from the garrisons at Jacob's, South Dublin Union, St. Stephen's Green and Boland's Mills.

Around 6:00AM, the British troops in the Shelbourne began firing upon the rebels below in St. Stephen's Green. The barrage was so intense that Commandant Mallin was forced to quickly evacuate the Green and flee to the nearby Royal College of Surgeons. Five rebels were killed in the Green and it became readily apparent that a major tactical blunder had occurred in making the Green a garrison without taking the hotel as well.

Meanwhile, at the GPO, work continued on strengthening the fortifications, the barricades and tunneling from building to building. The latter was part of James Connolly's strategy for urban warfare enabling personnel to move within buildings unseen and also as a safe method of communication.

At the same time, Patrick Pearse as President, issued the *"Irish War News"*, a newspaper issued by the Provisional Government. The purpose of the paper was to inform while maintaining the morale of the fighters. In the end, only one issue of the paper was ever printed.

On Tuesday afternoon, the British began the attack on the South Dublin Union. This was the result of probably the best strategic decision reached by the Military Council in planning the Rising.

The military headquarters of the British in Dublin was at the Royal Hospital in Kilmainham. Also, a major British garrison was housed at Richmond Barracks. Any movement by the British from the West would necessitate using the route Mount Brown/James Street. The South Dublin Union was fronted by James Street. Naturally, as the British moved toward the city center, they would meet determined resistance from the Union. The British decided to take the garrison rather than affect a by-pass.

In its initial assault, the British attempted to envelope the rebels by attacking from the rear (Rialto Bridge area) as well as from the front

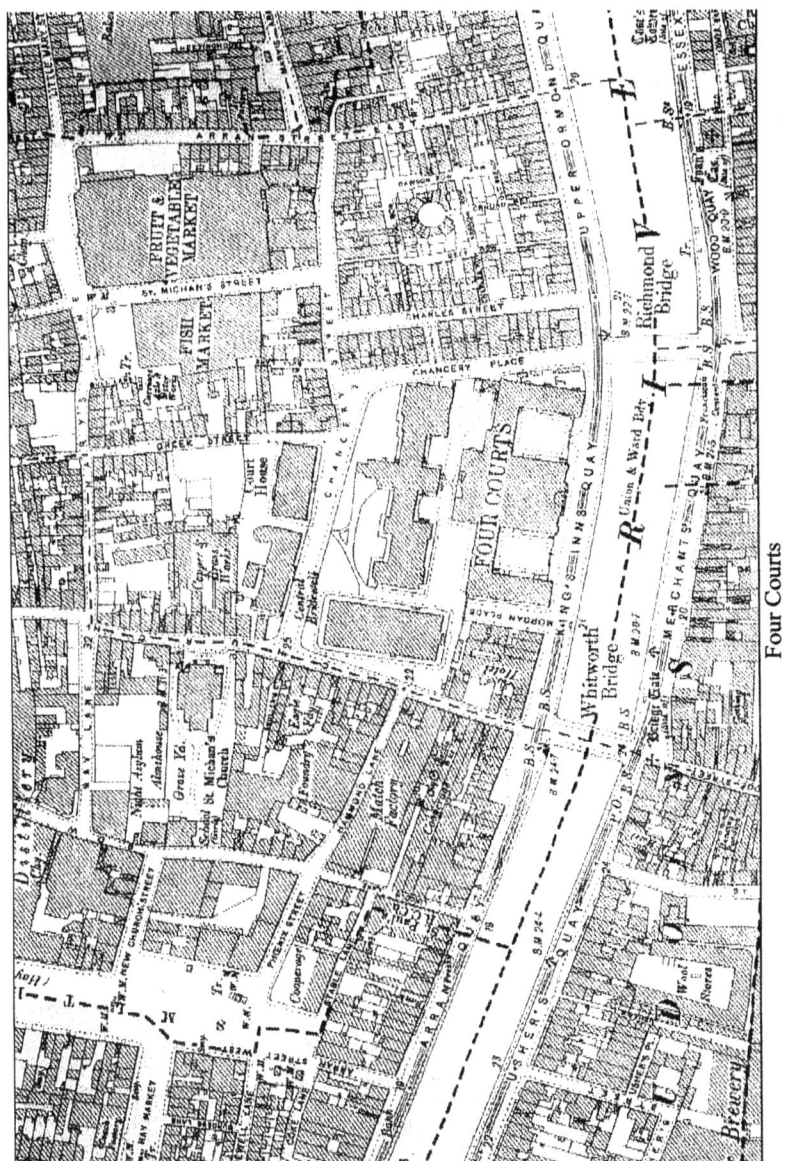

Four Courts

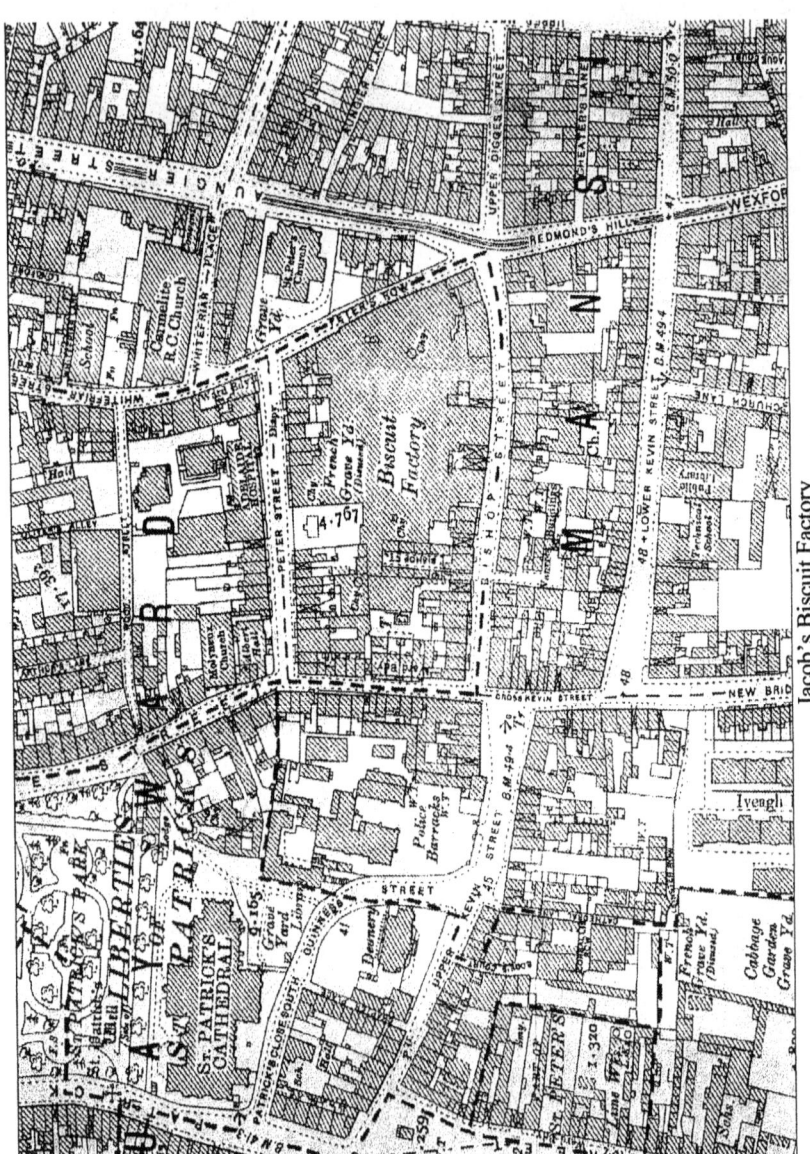

Jacob's Biscuit Factory

(James Street). At the same time, withering fire was maintained upon the Union from the Royal Hospital. By Tuesday evening, the Fourth Battalion was still in control of the entire South Dublin Union as well as its outposts on Marrowbone Lane and Ardee Street.

During the day on Tuesday, the British also attempted to force their way into the city from the Northwest, bringing troops from Marlborough and the Royal Barracks. These troops marched along the Quays on the North side of the Liffey. The very small post at the Mendicity Institution under Sean Heuston which was asked to maintain its position 'for a couple of hours' on Monday, successfully prevented those troops from advancing beyond Ellis and Arran Quay until Wednesday.

By Tuesday evening, the British had begun to appreciate the task before them. Reinforcements had begun to arrive, the Southern portion of a cordon had been established, and artillery had been requested to reduce the rebel garrisons. Looting around the GPO continued and civilian life had become difficult.

WEDNESDAY, APRIL 26

By Wednesday, the British had a clear strategy with their forces augmented by both troops and artillery. James Connolly, in his socialist thinking, was absolutely certain that capitalists (the British) would never destroy property with artillery. He had based his military preparations upon that belief and he was about to be proved wrong.

Early in the morning, the gunboat *Helga* sailed up the Liffey and began shelling Liberty Hall. Owing to the presence of Butts Bridge, however, it took most of the day to even hit the building. Liberty Hall had been deserted since Monday so that British efforts were wasted. Later in the day, the *Helga* sailed back down the Liffey and took time to shell the Boland's garrison. Commandant deValera had a flag posted on an unoccupied tower and the ruse allowed the British to shell another unimportant building, sparing the Boland's garrison any damage.

By noon, Sean Heuston's force of fifteen or so *Fianna* boys had held the British at bay for two days. His position had become untenable and it had little ammunition. He requested permission from headquarters to either evacuate or surrender, but no word was received as the British had completely isolated the position. With no recourse, Sean Heuston surrendered his force. The British were utterly astounded as to the age and the small size of the force which had prevented their advance for two days.

At around 2:30PM, the outposts of the Third Battalion along Pembroke and Northumberland Roads began to feel the pressure of the British reinforcements which had arrived in Ireland, landing at Kingstown. The particular unit advancing towards the Grand Canal bridge at Lower Mount Street was the Sherwood Foresters. The soldiers had been greeted enthusiastically during their march to the city by the citizens along the way. Things became very different when they reached the junction of Haddington Road and Northumberland Road.

The Foresters were under strict orders to follow the most direct route of march from Kingstown to Trinity College. That meant that when they reached the fork at Pembroke and Shelbourne Roads, their orders dictated that they follow the Pembroke route. Upon passing #25 Northumberland Road, they incurred enfilading fire from that location as well as fire from the school on the opposite side of the street, and a deadly barrage from the Clanwilliam House directly in front of them across Mount Street Bridge (officially named McKenny Bridge). Instead of retreating, or finding another way to cross the Grand Canal, they continued their suicidal frontal assault with devastating results. By late afternoon, the British had suffered over 200 dead and hundreds more casualties at this city block. The amazing aspect of the entire engagement was that the rebels had less than **TEN MEN** holding the three positions which defended this entry point to the city. By the time the battle was over, three of the defenders had escaped alive.

Meanwhile, the British had brought up artillery to begin their attack upon the Sackville Street area in general and the GPO in particular. Early in the day, the attacks had been concentrated upon Kelly's Fishing Tackle Shop located at the corner of Sackville Street and Bachelor's Walk. That position was lightly defended by the rebels, but it offered an outstanding sniper position for both sides of the river.

After silencing 'Fort Kelly', the British positioned artillery pieces in D'Olier Street aimed towards the GPO. Once again it took a great deal of time to find the correct range. Also, the pieces could not be well anchored into the street as the paving stones proved difficult to remove and they were not a proper base for the guns.

Wednesday had been a day when the spirit of the rebels had not diminished. Sean Heuston had held his position much longer than anyone had expected, and the engagement at Mount Street Bridge had proven disastrous for the British. On the other hand, ominous signs in the form of artillery began to appear and the leadership of the Rising was under no illusions regarding the outcome.

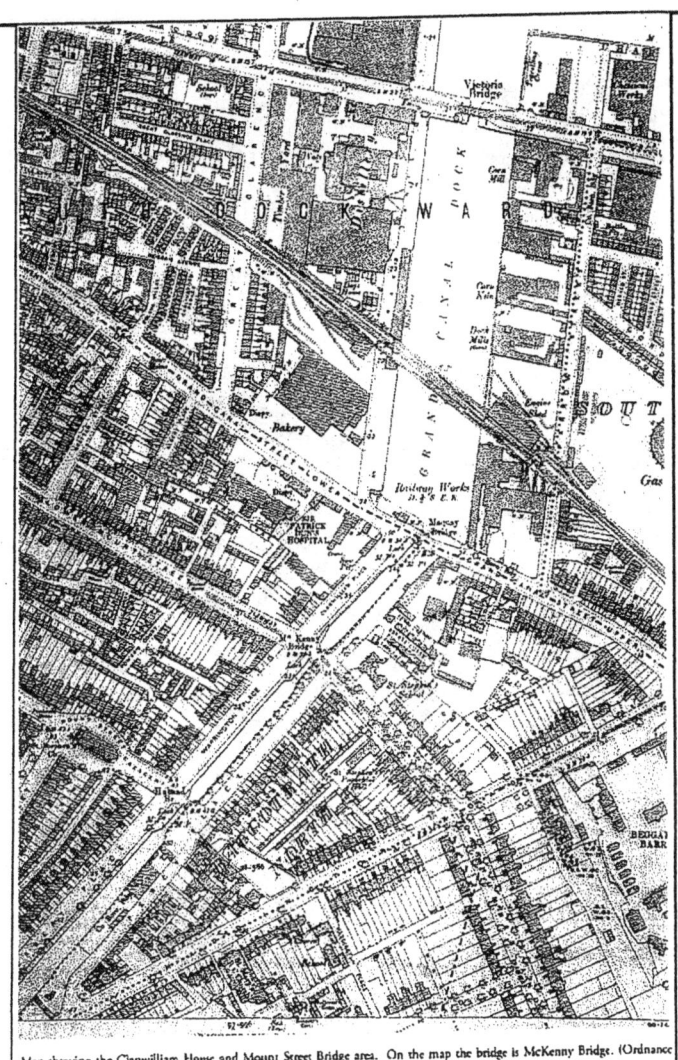

Map showing the Clanwilliam House and Mount Street Bridge area. On the map the bridge is McKenny Bridge. (Ordnance Survey, 1:2,500 (25 inches to mile), Dublin, sheet XVIII, 1911; scale altered).

Boland's- Mount Street

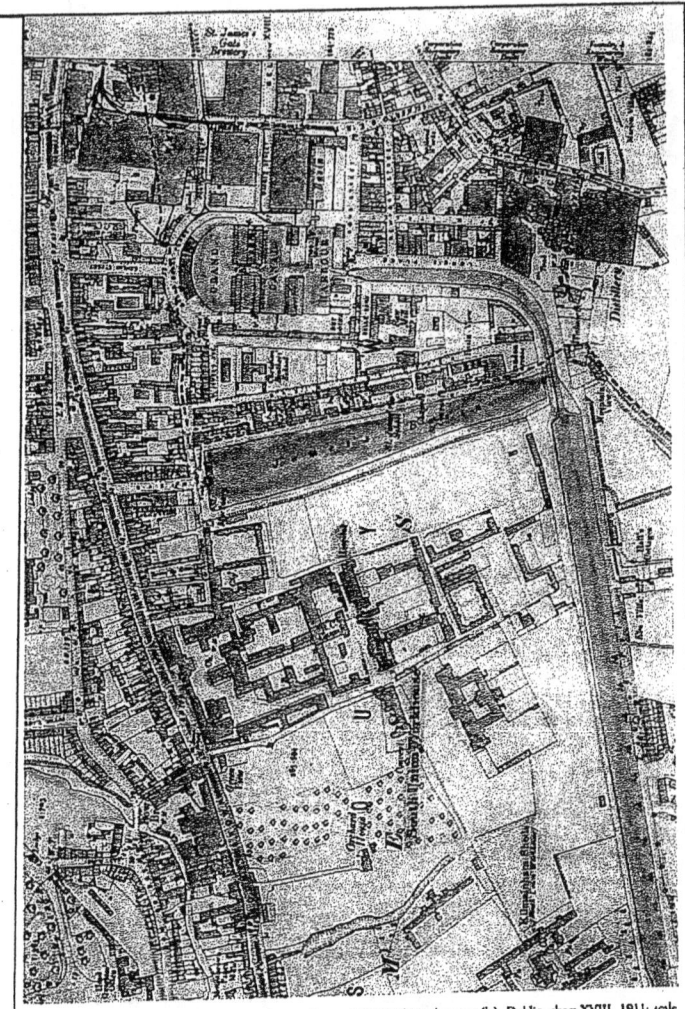

Map showing the South Dublin Union. (Ordnance Survey, 1:2,500 (25 inches to mile), Dublin, sheet XVIII, 1911; scale altered).

South Dublin Union

THURSDAY, APRIL 27

By Thursday morning, the British had begun to concentrate both their artillery and infantry fire upon Sackville Street. Much of the area began to show the destruction wrought by the British and there were numerous fires. In this area of operations, James Connolly recognized that subsequent to the 'softening up' exercise by the British, an all-out infantry assault would probably ensue. Toward that end, he made two fateful trips outside of the GPO.

Connolly's intention had been to check troop dispositions and the conditions of the various barricades. During the morning, he was checking a barricade on Sackville Street, when apparently satisfied, he excused himself from the officer in charge there and returned to the GPO. He asked the medical officer in the GPO to accompany him to a side room where he revealed a bullet wound in his arm and asked that it be dressed. He then ordered the man to secrecy about the injury as to not alarm the garrison.

As James Connolly was a man of incredible courage, he again ventured out of the GPO and took a detachment of rebels to Middle Abbey Street for tactical placement. As a matter of regular course, he made no attempt to cover himself, but demonstrated to his troops his disdain for danger. Upon his return to the GPO, a sniper's bullet ricochet seriously wounded him in the ankle after bouncing off the street. Unable to walk and bleeding profusely, he had to crawl all the way back to the GPO. A testament to his strength and determination was the fact that he did reach the GPO on his own.

Because of the foregoing, James Connolly was unable to perform the duties of military commander at different intervals during the next three days.

Elsewhere on Thursday, the British began their assault in earnest upon the South Dublin Union garrison. Owing to the vastness of the complex, actual fighting was mostly hand to hand. Soldiers on both sides battled from building to building, floor to floor, and in many cases, room to room. It was on this day that Commandant Ceannt's second in command, Cathal Brugha, made his epic 'last stand' against the British.

Brugha and his men had been fighting off a particularly ferocious British assault, when fearing that they were about to be overrun, he ordered his men to retreat. He remained as a rearguard. The British assaulted the position again and all firing stopped. Brugha's men reported to Ceannt what had occurred and all agreed that Cathal Brugha had surely died. A while later, Commandant Ceannt prepared to order a further retreat when one of his men reported hearing a very low voice singing from the area they had abandoned earlier in the day. Upon investigating, they found Cathal Brugha propped up against a wall singing patriotic songs and challenging the British to strike yet again. They carried Brugha back with them and subsequent investigation revealed that he had sustained twenty eight gunshot wounds.

By nightfall, Sackville Street was nearly engulfed in flames. Dublin civilians were suffering dreadfully as shops and services had been shut down for four days. The British had tightened their cordon around both the GPO area and the Four Courts. James Connolly was in critical condition as his wound had become infected. There was little effective anesthetic available and he had to endure great suffering with no rest.

All in the GPO were aware that the final assault would probably occur on the morrow, a prospect repeated for the South Dublin Union.

FRIDAY, APRIL 28

On Friday morning, the new British commander, Sir John Maxwell, arrived to take control of the response to the Easter Rising. The assault continued on Sackville Street, and by the afternoon, the roof of the GPO was burning. It became obvious to the leadership that the GPO would have to be evacuated.

A plan was devised whereby the garrison would vacate the GPO via Henry Street and establish a new headquarters. The side streets, being narrow and filled with smoke and debris, seemed to offer the best route of escape. Owing however, to little hard intelligence, the inability to physically observe and the incapacitance of James Connolly, the rebels had no real indication of what awaited them as they turned from Henry Street onto Moore Street.

The British cordon had tightened on the North side of the GPO to Parnell Street and at its intersection with Moore Street and a barricade erected there protected by machine guns. After a discussion among the leadership, it was agreed that a detachment under the leadership of The O'Rahilly (who volunteered to lead the group) would assault Moore Street and remove any barriers so that the main party could escape by that route. As O'Rahilly's group made the turn onto Moore Street, they came under intense machine gun fire. Many of the men huddled in doorways for they could not move in either direction. The O'Rahilly, seeing their position as hopeless, charged across Moore Street, suffered multiple wounds and dragged himself into a doorway at Sackville Lane.

As no one could get to him, he laid there all night. Sometime during that period, he dipped his finger into his own blood and wrote his name on the doorway beside his head.

Pearse ordered all of the women and the casualties removed from the GPO and taken towards Jervis Street Hospital. All obeyed except for four: James Connolly from his stretcher refused, his secretary, Winifred Carney refused to leave Connolly's side, and two nurses, Julia Grenan and Elizabeth O'Farrell refused to leave. Pearse checked the burning GPO to insure that everyone had left, and then he followed the rest to a grocery shop on the corner of Henry Street and Moore Street. James Connolly, of course, had to be carried on a stretcher. As elsewhere during the Rising, tunneling commenced immediately on Moore Street and headquarters was finally established at a fish shop at 16 Moore Street where the remnants of the GPO garrison spent Friday evening.

Meanwhile, intense fighting took place in the King Street North area, close to the Church Street intersection. In that vicinity, Commandant Daly had established very strong barricades at both Church Street and at King Street North. The rebels had also fortified many of the buildings in the area. The most famous of these was 'Reilly's Fort', a pub on the northwest corner of the intersection. In their assault, the British attempted to clear the area by starting at Beresford Street and moving west up King Street North. The distance needed to finalize the assault was about seventy five yards. Throughout Friday afternoon, the British pressed forward their attack, but to no avail. The battle was so intense that during Friday night, some of the British soldiers suffered mental breakdown. They broke into houses and murdered fifteen innocent civilians. The British continued the attack on 'Reilly's Fort' until Saturday morning. By that time, the rebels had withdrawn from the position.

The situation at the end of Friday was that the rebel leadership had abandoned their GPO headquarters and were on the run, the GPO itself was a gutted ruin, Sackville Street from Earl Street North to the Quays had been blasted and burned to the ground, the Four Courts garrison had been reduced to a small section of Church Street and atrocities had been committed against civilians by the British soldiers. On the other hand, the garrisons at Boland's Mills, the Royal College of Surgeons, South Dublin Union and Jacob's were still very capable of military action.

These functional garrisons, save for the South Dublin Union, had experienced little of the horrific mayhem which had befallen the GPO and the Four Courts area.

SATURDAY, APRIL 29

On the morning of the 29th, Pearse, McDermott and Clarke gathered around James Connolly's stretcher in Hanlon's Fish Shop, 16 Moore Street, to discuss their situation. Further movement for them was no longer possible. There were dead civilians on the pavement of Moore Street. By noon, it was decided that the Rising should end and that surrender was the only sane option which remained. Pearse had to find someway to contact the British for terms. It was decided that one of the women, Elizabeth O'Farrell, would carry a white flag and approach the barricade at the intersection of Moore and Parnell Streets.

She was taken by the British to General Lowe who said that no terms other than unconditional surrender would be offered. Nurse O'Farrell returned to 16 Moore Street and Pearse accepted the conditions. He stated that he did this to spare the city and its population any further harm or destruction. Perase formally surrendered to General Lowe at 2:30PM. He was then taken to General Maxwell where he was directed to pen surrender notes which could be presented to the remaining garrisons.

With Pearse's notes, Nurse O'Farrell was dispatched by the British to deliver the orders. Throughout Saturday afternoon, the remaining garrisons surrendered one at a time. Many of the rank and file rebels were bitter and considered not obeying the surrender orders. By that evening, however, reason had prevailed and the rebels were marched to the Rotunda Hospital at the top of Sackville Street where they were held in the open overnight. On Sunday morning, they were marched through the poorer areas of Dublin's streets where they were heckled by the local population. Eventually, they reached Richmond Barracks where they were incarcerated to await trial.

AFTERMATH

The Easter Rising had brought large scale death and destruction to Dublin. According to some sources[1], the death toll exceeded 400, while injuries to civilians were more than 2000, The lower portion of Sackville Street had been completely destroyed as had the adjacent streets. The general population of the city had been injured, displaced, inconvenienced and displeased by the events of Easter Week. As a consequence, the rebels were mostly condemned by the locals.

---

[1] Kiberd, Declan (Ed) 1916 Easter Rebellion Handbook, Mourne River, Dublin, 1998, pp. 49-50.

General Maxwell had decided to pursue a very strong and swift response to the leaders of the Rising. Not only would trials be done by military tribunals, they were to be carried out with unusual speed. Punishments were to be harsh and immediate.

Toward that end, court martials were conducted and concluded by May 3rd, with the results that fifteen rebel leaders were executed by May 12th. The seven signatories of the Proclamation of the Republic of Ireland were put to death along with Ned Daly, Michael O'Hanrahan, Willie Pearse, John MacBride, Con Colbert, Michale Mallin, Sean Heuston and Thomas Kent (executed at Cork, May 9th).

Because of the brutality of the executions, particularly Willie Pearse, and especially James Connolly, public opinion began to evolve to the side of the rebels. The fourteen executed at Kilmainham were all dumped into a hole filled with quicklime in a lot behind Arbour Hill Prison. None of the families, therefore, were allowed to claim the bodies for a proper Christian burial.

General Maxwell also ordered the arrest and imprisonment of a further 3226 people thought to have taken part or were in sympathy with the Rising. All were investigated and 1200 were held through June. The remaining, including five women, were dispatched to prisons in England.

The execution, incarcerations on non-participants, and the killing of innocent civilians all added to the eventual change of sympathy by the Irish people towards the rebels. The revelations did not occur immediately, but when the facts became known to the public, the rebels turned from anarchists in the minds of the people to heroes. The bravery of Cathal Brugha, the murder of Francis Sheehy-Skeffington, the marriage of Joseph Plunkett and Grace Gifford and similar facts assisted the rebels' cause in the inspiration caused by the Easter Rising for the concept of Irish independence.

Easter Rising Sites:
Dublin 1916 & Today

Site	Location	Use 1916	Today
General Post Office	O'Connell St	post office	post office
Dublin Castle	Dame St.	HQ British	museum
Boland's Mills	Grand Canal Quay	flour mill	same
Four Courts	Inn's Quay	records	records
St. Stephen's Green	Lesson-Grafton	city park	city park
Jacob's Biscuit Factory	Bishop St.	baked goods	archives
South Dublin Union	James St.	hospital	hospital
Mount Street Bridge	Mount St	bridge	bridge

Name Changes:

Royal Barracks	Benburb St	Collins Barracks	museum
Marlborough Barracks	Blackhorse Ave.	McKee Barracks	barracks
Richmond Barracks	Emmet Road	St. Michael's	school
Island Bridge Barracks	S Circular Rd.	Clancy Barracks	barracks
Wellington Barracks	S Circular Rd.	Griffith College	college
Potrobello Barrcaks	Rathmines	C Brugha Barracks	
Linenhall Barracks	Church St.	Technology	college
Ship Street Barracks	Ship St.		
Beggar's Bush Barracks	Haddington Rd.	Beggar's Bush	barracks

Railroad Terminals:

Amiens St. Sta.	Amiens St.	Connolly Station
Westland Row Sta.	Pearse St.	Pearse Station
Kingsbridge Sta.	St. John's Rd.	Heuston Station
Broadstone Sta.	Phibsborough	Bus Eireann
Harcourt St. Sta.	Harcourt St.	(Demolished)

Four Courts

GPO

Mount Street Bridge & Clanwilliam House

Mount Street Bridge

25 Northumberland Road

Liberty Hall

Gravesites

Ashe, Thomas	Glasnevin
Brugha, Cathal	Glasnevin
Casement, Sir Roger	Glasnevin
Ceannt, Eamonn	Arbour Hill
Clarke, Thomas	Arbour Hill
Colbert, Con	Arbour Hill
Collins, Michael	Glasnevin
Connolly, James	Arbour Hill
Daly, Edward	Arbour Hill
deValera, Eamonn	Glasnevin
Heuston, Sean	Arbour Hill
Kearney, Peadar	Glasnevin
MacBride, John	Arbour Hill
MacDonagh, Thomas	Arbour Hill
Mallin, Michael	Arbour Hill
Markievicz, Constance	Glasnevin
McDermott, Sean	Arbour Hill
O'Rahilly, The	Glasnevin
Pearse, Patrick	Arbour Hill
Pearse, William	Arbour Hill
Plunkett, Joseph	Arbour Hill

Arbour Hill Cemetery- Dublin

Thomas Clarke marker-
Arbour Hill Cemetery

Cathal Brugha

Roger Casement

Michael Collins

Eamonn deValera

Countess Constance Markievicz

The O'Rahilly

Maud Gonne MacBride

CASUALTIES
{source: The Easter Rebellion Handbook,
Ed. Declan Kibberd, Mourne Press, 1998, pp. 51-59}

It was very difficult to get an accurate accounting of casualties attributable directly to the Easter Rising, particularly civilian deaths. This source lists the names of all killed and wounded of the British forces and the Irish polices forces. There is also a list of dead for the rebels.

The listing for civilian deaths offers names, addresses and places of burial, but the numbers do not agree with the totals listed on the main chart.

Official List of Casualties

Type	Killed	Wounded	Missing	Total
Military officers	17	46		63
Military others	86	311	9	406
RIC officers	2			2
RIC others	12	23		35
Dublin police	3	3		6
Civilians & Insurgents	180	614	—	794
TOTAL:	300	997	9	1306

Persons interred in Dublin cemeteries between Easter and July 11, 1916:

Glasnevin	250
Mount Jerome	24
Dean's Grange	49

BRITISH & POLICE DEATHS

Sherwood Foresters	24
South Staffordshire	15
North Staffordshire	2
Royal Irish Rifles	9
Royal Irish Fusiliers	11
Royal Irish Regiment	7
Royal Inniskilling Fusiliers	1
Leinster Regiment	1
Army Service Corps	3
Royal Field Artillery	1
Lancers	9
Hussars	6
Yeomanry	3
2nd King Edward's	1
Naval Detachment	1
Royal Irish Constabulary	14
Dublin Metropolitan Police	3
1st Volunteer Training Corps	5

Volunteer & Citizen Army Killed

Adams, John	Dwan, John
Allen, Thomas	Ennis, Edward
Burke, Frank	Farrell, Patrick
Byrne, Andrew	Fox, James
Byrne, James	Geoghegan, George
Byrne, Joseph	Healy, John
Carrigan, Charles	Howard, Sean
Clarke, Philip	Hurley, John
Connolly, Sean	Kealy, John
Corcoran, James	Kent, Richard
Costello, John	Keogh, Richard
Coyle, Harry	Macken, Francis
Crinigan, John	Macken, Peter
Cromean, John	Malone, Michael
Darcy, Charles	Manning, Peter
Darcy, Peter	McCormack, J.
Donelan, Brandan	M'Dowell, William
Doyle, Patrick	Murphy, D

Murphy, Richard

Murray, D.

O'Carroll, Richard

O'Flanagan, Peter

O'Grady, John

O'Rahilly, The

O'Reilly, J.

O'Reilly, Richard

O'Reilly, Thomas

Owens, J

Quinn, James

Rafferty, Thomas

Reynolds, George

Ryan, Frank

Sheehan, Domhnall

Traynor, John

Walsh, Edward

Weafer, Thomas

Whelan, Patrick

Wilson, Peter

SIDEBAR: The Destruction in Dublin

A. Hibernian Fire & General Insurance Company map
   (Source: *1916 The Easter Rising*, Tim Pat Coogan, Cassall, 2001)

According to the above source, this map was issued shortly after the Easter Rising and shows the extent of damage upon the Sackville Street of Dublin.

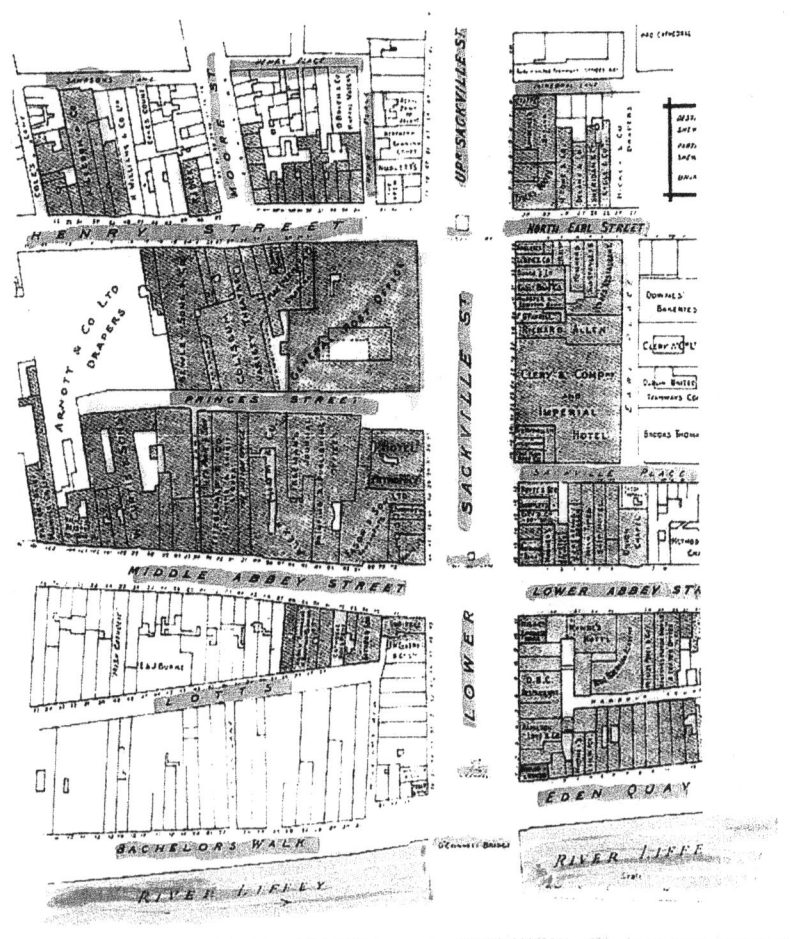

"Well-known Houses Destroyed & Damaged"

Source: *The Easter Rebellion Handbook*, Mourne River, 1998, p 32

" A representative of the *Weekly Irish Times* complied a list of houses which had been destroyed by fire in the central streets of Dublin. In the case of many houses, only the name of the chief firm doing business there is given; and other persons have offices or rooms in the building as well. In some instances the premises are only partially destroyed.

The rateable annual value of the properties set out in this list, based upon the new valuations given in *Thom's Directory* for 1916, exclusive of any estimate for stocks of goods in the different premises, and also excluding any figure for the General Post Office, the Royal Hibernian Academy, the Presbyterian Union Chapel, or the Methodist Church in Abbey Street amounts to 241,870 English pounds"

PROPERTIES DESTROYED DURING THE EASTER RISING
[Source: The Easter Rebellion Handbook, Mourne River, 1998, pp 27-34]

LOWER SACKVILLE STREET

No.	Occupant	Trade
1	Hopkins & Hopkins	jewellers
2	William Scott & Co.	tailors
3	Hamilton, Long & Co.	apothecaries
4	Francis Smyth & Son	umbrella manufacturers
5	The Waverley Hotel	
6	Great Western Railway of England	
6-7	Dublin Bread Company	
	Frank R. Gallagher	cigar merchant
8	Grand Hotel & Restaurant	
9	ER Moore	jeweller
10-11	Charles L. Reis & Co.	fancy goods warehouse
	The Irish School of Wireless Telegraphy	
12-13	The Hibernian Bank	
14	Robert Buckham	gentlemen's outfitter
15	City & County Permanent Building Society	
16	F Sharpley	ladies/children's outfitters
17	Hoyte & Son	druggists
	GP Beater	architect
18	The True Form Boot Company	
19	JP Callahan	tailor and hosier
20	George Mitchell	cigar and wine merchant
21-27	The Imperial Hotel	
	Clery & Company	drapers
28	Richard Allen	tailor
29	Frs O'Farrell	tobacco importer
30	The Munster and Leinster Bank	
31	The Cable Boot Comany	
32	Dunn & Co.	hatters
33	Lewers and Co.	boys' clothiers
34	Noblett's Ltd.	
35	Kapp and Peterson	tobacconists
35-39	Hotel Metropole	
39	Henry Gandy	tailor
40	Eason and Sons	general newspaper
41	David Drimmie & Sons	insurance
42	The Misses Carolan	milliners
43-44	Manfield & Sons	boots and shoes
46-47	John W. Elvery and Co.	

UPPER SACKVILLE STREET

No.	Occupant	Trade
1	John Tyler & Sons	boot merchants
2	Dublin Laundry Co.	
3	John McDowell	jeweller
4	E Nestor	milliner
5-7	William Lawrence	photographer
8	Henry Taaffe	gentleman's outfitter

SACKVILLE PLACE

No.	Occupant	Trade
11	vacant	
13	Corrigan & Wilson	printers
14	John Devin	
16	Denis J. Egan	wine & spirits merchant

HENRY STREET

No.	Occupant	Trade
6	Samuel Samuels	jewellers
16	James O'Dwyer and Co.	tailors
17	Harrison and Co.	cooks and confectioners
18-20	Bewley, Sons and Co.	provisions
21	Irish Farm Produce Co.	
22-23	E. Morris	merchant tailor
24	The Coliseum Theatre	
25	HE Randall	boot and shoe makers
26-26	Mcinvernoy & Co.	drapers
27	McDowell Brothers	jewellers
29	Adelaide Repleto	fancy warehouse
30	The World's Fair 6 1/2d Stores	
34	Dundon and Co.	tailors
35	A Clarke and Co.	millinery
36	Madame Drago	hairdresser
37	E Marks and Co.	Penny Bazaar
38	R and J Wilson and Co.	confectioners
39	McCarthy and Co.	costume and mantle
40	Bailey Brothers	tailors
40a	Mrs. Charlotte Gahagan	ladies outfitter
41a	Joseph Calvert	provision merchant
41	Patrick M'Givney	cutler & optician
42	John Murphy	spirits merchant
43	R and J Dick	boots and shoes
44	Caroline E Fegan and Co.	underclothing
49	Menzies and Co.	milliners
50	Hampton, Leedom and Co.	hardware merchants
51	Hayes, Conyngham and Robinson	chemists
52	Miss White	milliner
53	Maples and Co.	tailors

LOWER ABBEY STREET

No.	Occupant	Trade
1	Young & Co. Ltd	wine and spirits
2	JJ Kelly and Co.	cycle agents
3	JJ Keating	cycle and motor dealers
4	Irish Times, Ltd.	
5	Ship Hotel and Tavern	
6	The Abbey Toilet Saloon, Ltd	
7	John Hyland and Co.	wine merchant
8	KG Henry	tobacconist
	Presbyterian Church	Rev. Johnston minister
23	Patrick Foley	wine and spirits
29	Denis Nolan	private hotel
30	Francis Marnane	furrier
31	William Collins	oil importer
32	Humber, Ltd	cycle and motor
	The Leader	newspaper
32-33	Keating's Motor Works	
	The Irish Commercial Travellers' Assn	
33-34	Percy, Macready and Co.	publishers
	Irish Homestead Publishing Co.	
	James M'Cullagh & Sons	wine merchants
	Royal Hibernian Academy	
35-37	Wynn's Hotel	
37	Smyth & Co.	hosiery mfg.
38	JJ Ferguson & Co.	hair dressers
39	Peter Callaghan	gentleman's outfitter

PROPERTIES DESTROYED DURING THE EASTER RISING
(Source: The Easter Rebellion Handbook, Mourne River, 1998, pp 32-34)

MIDDLE ABBEY STREET

No.	Occupant	trade
62	Patrick Gordon	wine merchant
66	WJ Haddock	tailor
67	Collins & Co.	tailors
68	George Young	ironmongers
69-70	Sharman Crawford	wine merchant
71	Dermot Dignam	advertising agent
73	James Allen & Sons	auctioneers
74-75	Gaynor & Son	cork merchants
76	YMCA	
78	John J Egan	wine and spirit merchant
	The Oval	
79-82	Eason and Son, Ltd.	wholesale newsagents
83	The Evening Telegraph	
84	Weekly Freeman and Sport	
85	Sullivan Brothers	educational publishers
86	Sealy, Bryers, and Walker	printers
87-90	Alexander Thom and Co.	gov't printers
91-93	Fitzgerald & Co.	tea, wine and spirit
94	The Wallpaper Manufacturing Co.	
96	Maunsel and Co.	publishers
	Francis Tucker and Co., Ltd	church candles
97	W Dawson and Sons, Ltd	wholesale agents
98-99	W Curtis & Sons	brass and bell founders
100	J Whitby and Co.	cork merchants
101	John Kane	art metal worker
102-04	National Reserve Headquarters	
105	Perfect Dairy Machine Co.	

EARL STREET

No.	Occupant	trade
1a	James Tallon	newsagent
1	T Carson	tobacconist
2	A Sullivan	confectionist
3	JJ Lalor	Catholic art repository
4	Philip Meagher	vitner
5	James Winstanley	boot warehouse
6	Noreau et Cie	costumiers
7	Sir Joseph Downes	confectioner
25	J Nagle and Co.	wine merchant
26	Mrs. E Sheridan	wine and spirit
27	Dealney and Co.	tobacco and cigars
27a	J Alexander	merchant tailor
28	M Rowe and Co.	general drapers
29-31	John Tyler & Sons	boot manufacturers

PRINCE'S STREET

No.	Occupant	trade
3	Princes Stores	
4-8	Freeman's Journal	
13	Stores	
14	vacant	
15	Pirie and Sons	stores

HARCOURT STREET

No.	Occupant	trade
96	Norma Reeves	tailor
97a	Mrs. Elizabeth Bryan	fruiterer

EDEN QUAY

No.	Occupant	trade
1-2	Barry, O'Moore & Co.	accountants
3	Gerald Mooney	wine and spirit
4	The London & Northwest Railway Co.	
5	GR Mesios	military tailor
6	The Midland Railway of England	
	Wells and Holohan	shipping agents
7	J. Hubbard Clark	painter and decorator
8	The Globe Parcel Express	
9	Henry Smith Ltd	ironmonger
10	Joseph M'Greavy	wine and spirit
11	The Douglas Hotel and Restaurant	
12	Mr. John Dalby	
13	The Mission to Seamen Institute	
14	E Moore	publican

MOORE STREET

No.	Occupant	trade
1-2	J Huraphrys	wine and spirit
3	O Savino	fried fish shop
4	Miss B Morris	dairy
5	MJ Dunne	pork butcher
6	R Dillon	fruiterer
59	Francis Fee	wine and spirit
60	Miss M'Nally	greengrocer
61	K O'Donnell	victualler
62	Miss Ward	victualler

LOWER BRIDGE STREET

No.	Occupant	trade
18	tenements	
19-21	Doherty's Hotel	
20	Brazen Head Hotel	

USHER'S QUAY

No.	Occupant	trade
1	H Kavanaugh	wine and spirit
2-3	Dublin Clothing Co.	
4	tenements	

BOLTON STREET

No.	Occupant	trade
57	George Freyne	hardward merchant
58	D Dolan	chemist
59	W Leckie & Co	printers
60	tenements	

MARLBOROUGH STREET

No.	Occupant	trade
112	J Farrell	wine and spirit
113	Marlborough Hotel	

CLANWILLIAM PLACE

No.	Occupant	trade
1-2	private houses	

YARNHALL STREET

No.	Occupant	trade
1	Hugh, Moore & Alexanders	druggists
	Linenhall Barracks	
4-7	W Leckie & Co.	workshops

BERESFORD PLACE

No.	Occupant	trade
16-17	Liberty Hall	IGTWU headquarters

SELECTED COURT MARTIAL RESULTS
{source: The Easter Rebellion Handbook,
Ed. Declan Kibberd, Mourne Press, 1998, pp. 51-59}

NAME	SENTENCE	RESULT
Patrick Pearse	death	executed May 3
Thomas MacDonagh	death	executed May 3
Thomas Clarke	death	executed May 3
Joseph Plunkett	death	executed May 4
Michael O'Hanrahan	death	executed May 4
Edward Daly	death	executed May 4
William Pearse	death	executed May 4
Bevan, Thomas	death	commuted 10 years
Tobin, William	death	commuted 10 years
Walsh, Thomas	death	commuted 10 years
Irvine, George	death	commuted 10 years
Lynch, Finian	death	commuted 10 years
Doherty, John	death	commuted 10 years
Mervyn, Michael	death	commuted 10 years
Walsh, JJ	death	commuted 10 years
O'Callaghhan, Dennis	death	commuted 10 years
Sweeney, P.E.	death	commuted 10 years
Reid, J.J.	death	commuted 10 years
McNestry, Patrick	death	commuted 10 years

Williams, John	death	commuted 10 years
Hunter, Thomas	death	commuted life
MacBride, John	death	executed May 5
Cosgrove, William	death	commuted life
Beasley, Pierce	3 years	3 years
Markievicz, Constance	death	commuted life
Plunkett, George	death	commuted 10 years
Plunkett, John	death	commuted 10 years
Colbert, Cornelius	death	executed May 8
Kent, Edmund	death	executed May 8
Mallin, Michael	death	executed May 8
Heuston, J.J.	death	executed May 8
Kent, Thomas	death	executed May 9
deValera, Edward	death	commuted life
Boland, Henry	10 years	5 years remitted
Connolly, James	death	executed May 12
McDermott, John	death	executed May 12
MacNeill, John	life	life
Casement, Sir Roger	death	executed Aug. 3

PRISONERS DEPORTED

Summary: July 11, 1916

Total prisoners passed through Richmond Barracks: 3226

Men: 3149, Women: 77

Men released: 1104, Convicted by court martial: 160

Acquitted by court martial: 23

Interned- Men: 1852, Women: 5

DEPORTED PRISONERS

Where	Date	Number
Knutsford	May 1	200
Stafford	May 1	289
Knutsford	May 3	308
Wakefield	May 6	376
Stafford	May 8	203
Wandsworth	May 9	197
Wandsworth	May 13	54
Stafford	May 13	58
Wakefield	May 13	273
Glasgow & Perth	May 20	197
Woking	May 20	40
Lewes	May 20	59
Wakefield	June 2	100

Wandsworth	June 2	49
Knutsford	June 2	50
Kuntsford	June 7	41
Knutsford	June 16	25

Retained at Richmond Barracks.....................211

THE EXECUTIONS

April 1916

24	25	26 Easter Rising	27	28	29
←					→

May 1916

	1	2	3	4 Patrick Pearse Thos. MacDonagh Thomas Clarke	5 Joseph Plunkett Edward Daly Mick O'Hanrahan William Pearse	6 John MacBride
7	8 Con Colbert Eamonn Ceannt Michael Mallin Sean Heuston	9	10	11	12 James Connolly Sean McDermott	13

After the surrender, the rebels were held outside of the Rotunda Hospital overnight. From there, they were marched to Richmond Barracks for detention and sorting. James Connolly, however, remained at Dublin Castle as his wounds and condition made it impossible for him to be moved.

General Maxwell had already decided that justice would be both swift and harsh. Court martial would be the method of trial, the defendants would not be entitled to counsel, and a guilty verdict would be punishable by firing squad. His reasons were manifold i.e., he wished to eliminate the rebellious leadership, he wished the punishment be an example, and he wanted to exert and demonstrate complete British authority.

On Monday, May 1st, Patrick Perase was moved from Arbour Hill Prison to Richmond Barracks. He stood court martial that afternoon along with Thomas Clarke and Thomas MacDonagh. Each of them faced the three man court individually. All were found guilty and Maxwell issued the death sentences.

From Richmond, they were transferred to Kilmainham Gaol where the executions were to take place. Late in the evening, Thomas Clarke and Thomas MacDonagh were allowed short visits by family members. Thomas Clarke's wife, Kathleen (a sister of Commandant Ned Daly) was in the early stages of pregnancy of which her husband was unaware, and of which she did not wish to concern him (she suffered a miscarriage shortly thereafter). Pearse was supposed to receive a visit from his mother, but the British could not get her safely from Rathfarnham to Kilmainham.

During the afternoon of Tuesday, May 2nd, court martials were carried out for William Pearse, Joseph Plunkett, Ned Daly and Michael O'Hanrahan. All of them were found guilty and sentenced to death.

Kilmainham Gaol

Stonebreaker's Yard

In the early hours of Wednesday, May 3rd, Clarke, MacDonagh and Pearse were executed in Stonebreaker's Yard at Kilmainham. Their bodies, like all of those to follow, were wrapped in blankets, put into an ambulance and taken to a yard at the rear of Arbour Hill Prison where they were buried in quicklime to insure that they decomposed quickly in a place where their remains were safely under British control.

Arbour Hill Cemetery

Later in the day, four more leaders were tried, found guilty, and sentenced to death: John MacBride, Michael Mallin, Sean Heuston and the Countess, Constance Markievicz. The latter expressed immense pride in her role during the Rising and insisted that she was quite prepared to die.

Again, early in the morning of Thursday, May 4th, the firing squads did their tasks. All of those executed, W. Pearse, Plunkett, Daly and O'Hanrahan were visited by family, administered by priests (from here on, the priests were allowed to witness the executions, unlike the first three) and shot in Stonebreaker's Yard. These bodies, too, were taken to Arbour Hill. Joseph Plunkett was allowed to marry Grace Gifford a couple of hours before his execution (see "The Marriage of Joseph Plunkett & Grace Gifford").

Later that day, Eamonn Ceannt and Con Colbert faced court martial, were found guilty and sentenced to death.

John MacBride's execution occurred on Saturday, May 6th, while Con Colbert, Michael Mallin, Sean Heuston and Eamonn Ceannt were executed on Monday morning, May 8th. In the meantime, the death sentence of Countess Markievicz had been, much to her dismay, commuted to life imprisonment because of her gender. Also, on May 9th, the court martial of Eamonn deValera took place. As a Commandant, he was found guilty and sentenced to death. However, as deValera had been born in the United States and lived the first two years of his life there, he was a U.S. citizen which created a problem for the British authorities. The U.S. Ambassador and deValera's mother were able to intervene and his sentence was commuted to life imprisonment. Eamonn deValera, therefore, was the only leader of the Easter Rising to survive, and, of course, this fact had a great impact in his ensuing political life as Ireland's greatest statesman in the 20th Century.

Meanwhile, James Connolly remained in very poor condition in Dublin Castle. His wounded ankle had developed gangrene and at that point he was probably dying. He had his court martial at the Castle. During the hearing, he had to be propped-up on a stretcher as he was unable to sit upright. After his guilty sentence, he was transferred by ambulance from the Castle to Kilmainham accompanied by Fr. Aloysius, Fr. Sebastian and Surgeon Tobin. In the early morning of Friday, May 12th, James Connolly was executed right after Sean McDermott. Connolly was the only rebel executed at the opposite end of the yard by the entrance gate. Because of his condition, James Connolly was strapped to a chair for his execution, and for that reason he was not carried to the other end.

Thus, within a period of twelve days, fourteen leaders of the Easter Rising had been executed, including all seven signatories of the Proclamation. General Maxwell had completed his task, but even before the last execution, public opinion had begun to turn in favor of the rebel It is worth noting that General Blackadder, one of the three members of the British military court holding the trials noted "I've just performed one of the hardest tasks I have ever had to do. Condemned to death one of the finest characters I ever came across. A man named Pearse. Must be something very wrong in the state of things, must there not that makes a man like that a rebel? I'm not surprised that his pupils adored him".[2]

Dublin Castle

---

[2] deRosa, Peter, Rebels, Ballantine, New York, 1990, p. 424.

Book Review

The Capuchin Annual 1966
Brother Henry, OFM. Cap
Church Street, Dublin
564 pps.

This is probably the most quoted work found in any book or article dealing with the Easter Rising of 1916. What makes this book even more extraordinary is that it was published by the Franciscan Capuchin Friars of Church Street, Dublin, the same order of priests from the same church who administered the final spiritual needs of the men executed at Kilmainham in May, 1916. Also, the friary is located just two blocks from North King Street, the scene of intense and infamous fighting. Also, the friary contained Fr. Matthew Hall which was used as a hospital by the Volunteers.

The book itself contains a series of twenty articles written by the people who experienced the Rising. Some of the articles were reprinted from The Capuchin Annual 1942 which commemorated the 25th Anniversary.

The articles themselves deal with all centers of rebel activity in the Dublin area including Ashbourne. They deal with the Volunteers, The Citizen Army, and the Cumann na mBan. Each is extremely well written and each is a full story unto itself.

Some of the writings explore the Easter Rising as it impacted Ireland beyond Dublin. The events in Enniscorthy, Galway, Limerick, Kerry, Cork and Belfast are individually described.

One of the things which make this volume unique is that it contains the "Personal Recollections" of Fr. Aloysius, OFM Cap., a letter from Fr. Augustine OFM Cap. regarding Con Colbert, and another article from Fr. Albert OFM Cap. that describes the final hours of Sean Heuston. These descriptions shed important light on the holiness and spirituality of the leaders of the Easter Rising which has been overlooked in other accounts.

The map on page 168 is excellent, one of the few to properly label Wellington Barracks as such and not as Richmond Barracks as frequently found in other references. The numerous photos contained in the work are also excellent; many of them are not found elsewhere. There are pictures of written documents which are very relevant to the text- these do not appear in other books.

One note of a personal nature: A serious student of The Easter Rising must consult this work to have a complete understanding of the events i.e., this is one of the two major works with total credibility (the other is Max Caulfield's <u>Easter Rebellion</u>). This book is *extremely rare* and very seldom available for purchase anywhere. If one has the opportunity to acquire a copy, do it, there will be no disappointment.

Book Review
The Easter Rebellion
Max Caulfield
Four Square, London 1963
380 pps.

This is the work about The Easter Rising to which all other are judged! The structure of the survey is site-based, i.e., events for the entire week in 1916 are given for each site in their entirety, rather than a day-to-day description of all events everywhere. This approach allows the reader a chance to digest the information and at the same time, stay with the participants long enough to get to know them.

Caulfield's work is also unique as it relies upon hundreds of witness statements which he gathered. Rather than merely assemble the work through literary research, he made it truly come alive with the memories of those who survived. Thus, there are instances where the commentary of the participants differ from the standard historical record. There are also numerous caveats not found elsewhere.

There are no photographs, but the maps are excellent. The book reads easily, but I would recommend it to someone who wishes to gain the most in-depth knowledge, and who has a prior understanding of The Easter Rising.

Interestingly, Caulfield's title probably rankled his Irish audience, but he adequately addresses that at the beginning of the book. He also shies away from using Gaelic names, but uses English equivalents throughout.

This is truly the classic narrative of The Easter Rising and should be read along with The Capuchin Annual 1966.

Book Review
The Rising
The Complete Story of Easter Week
Desmond Ryan
Golden Eagle, 1949- 1966 Edition

This book has been around for a great number of years and probably deserves more publicity than it currently deserves. The author was acquainted with many participants of The Easter Rising and was able to get their recollections into print well before the popular histories were written.

One must keep in mind that the work was completed in 1949, and that the edition above is from 1966, therefore, there are no photographs, nor is there an itemized bibliography. Reference citations are at the bottom of the individual pages. The only map available is on the inside of the front and back covers (the same map), again a method fashionable at the time of publication.

Putting aside the aesthetics of the presentation, the book is quite complete in that it traces the origins of The Easter Rising, continues with the confusion at the outset, and then, finally, begins a chapter by chapter site-based account of the entire week. I must confess that I found the first half of the book difficult as it meandered through many peripheral events which seemed to gain more space than the particular item may have merited e.g., Mendicity Institution is traced from its beginnings as Moira House through a couple of hundred years until it fulfils its role in the Rising. This is interesting, but not germane to the topic.

There is a wonderful description of Cathal Brugha's courageous defense at South Dublin Union. The event has been described often elsewhere, but it fits into the flow of the S.D.U. garrison better here than elsewhere.

If one were to begin a serious study of The Easter Rising, I would recommend reading this work at the beginning of the quest rather than later (as I did). It is my opinion that the later histories relied a great deal upon Ryan's work, but cut pieces from it and they do not convey the same meaning as they do in the original form. The shortcoming on no photographs can be easily served through use of the internet, or with Tim Pat Coogan's highly illustrated The Easter Rising.

Book Review
Witnesses: Inside the Easter Rising
Annie Ryan
Liberties Press, Dublin, 2005
224 pps.

This is a very interesting book as it is derived from an Irish Government effort to chronicle statements by participants of the Easter Rising. This was done in the 1940's and 1950's, but these archives were only released to the public in 2003.

The book itself is very well presented with the various organizations explained at the beginning along with short sketches of the main players. The reading moves very quickly as it take a chronological approach of moving through the events of the Rising.

There is an appropriate look at the role of women in the action. Many of the recollections, though not released for many years, have been well documented in other works, such as Frank Robbins. He gave his account to Max Caulfield for use in The Easter Rebellion. Nonetheless, much of the information is new and different, making the book somewhat unique.

At the end of the work, a complete list of witness statements which are available for research is given. This is a very useful tool for anyone planning on visiting the military Archives at Cathal Brugha Barracks.

The photos and the map are rather ordinary, but useful. I would recommend this book to any student of The Easter Rising.

Book Review
No Ordinary Women....Irish Female Activists
In the Revolutionary Years 1900-1923
Sinead McCoole
University of Wisconsin, Madison, 2003
280 pps.

This is a very lavishly illustrated presentation of the role of women in Ireland's struggle for independence from the founding of the various organizations through the Civil War.

Ms. McCoole has gathered a great deal of memorabilia and presented it along with pertinent descriptions making the book really come alive. Everything is here for both the interested first-timer to the veteran scholar. It traces the roots of the women's organizations, the key players in those roots, the role of women throughout the struggle, and the penal consequences for the women along the way.

There are basically five parts to the book: the organizations, the Rising, the War for Independence, the Civil War, and biographies. The first four are straight-line summaries of the events as they involved the women. The biography section is excellent in that it allows the reader a place to make a solid connection with the subject anytime during the use of the book.

The book also contains prisoner lists for both the Rising and the War for Independence, as well as an excellent map of the Rising in Dublin and a thorough bibliography.

The book absolutely ranks in my top three in dealing with Irish History in the period 1916-1923. It definitely in the best work about the role of women.

Book Review

A Walk through Rebel Dublin 1916
Mick O'Farrell
Mercier Press, Cork 1999
128 pps.

This is an excellent book in that it does exactly what it was intended to do, no more and certainly no less. As it is intended to be as much a guidebook as a historical survey, the concept of then and now works very well.

The historical photographs of the thirty sites have all been presented before in one form or another. The present-day pictures were taken at the same angles in most cases as the originals, offering wonderful points of reference.

There is a general map at the beginning of the book which is adequate, but smaller scale supplementary maps for each area would have been more helpful. Contemporary commentary for each site seems to have been taken from Max Caulfield and Desmond Ryan. The bibliography offers most standard accounts of the Rising except for Peter deRosa's Rebels, and Foy & Barton's The Easter Rising.

If a complaint can be made about this book, I think it would involve the presentation, in essence, the 7 ¾" by 5" size. For a work based first and foremost upon photographs, it would seem that a significantly larger size Page would lend itself better to readability. The cramped size also presents problems inside. The text is excellent, but very small. The pages are very full, suggesting that economy was a primary publishing concern. In order to read the caption of some of the photographs, one must strain to push open the book to find the words hidden down towards the spine.

I suppose that I would have had contemporary photographs in color; although the original photos being black and white, probably necessitated continuity. Also, although thirty sites have been presented, I cannot imagine why Arbour Hill Cemetery, Kilmainham Gaol and Richmond Barracks were not included. Perhaps Kilmainham Museum would not allow a contemporary presentation.

Finally, I would agree with Mr. O'Farrell about the fact that Dublin City does not do enough to signpost these very important historical sights. In my visits to Dublin, I once had to circle three times, asking directions each time before finding Arbour Hill Cemetery (and that was by accident!). That would be akin to visiting Washington D.C. and being unable to find Arlington National Cemetery.

Book Review
When History Was Made...
The Women of 1916
Ruth Taillon
Beyond the Pale Publications, Belfast, 1996
113 pps.

This work traces the significant involvement of women in the 1916 Easter Rising. It appears at first glance to be a timeframe from Margaret Ward's Unmanageable Revolutionaries . However, the work certainly has its own identity.

It begins with a complete list of women who were involved in the Rising, regardless of their capacity. This is very important as one realizes immediately that women were posted at all battle sites except Boland's.

The initial organizing of women begins the saga and traces the various groups from their early formation to their role in either the Cumann na mBan or Citizen Army. The origins and the various individuals are very important because the women, unlike the men, were not executed for their involvement, and were able to continue onward as most of the veterans of the Easter Rising were incarcerated.

There are excellent photographs in the book, some of which do not appear in other works about the Rising. The only problem with the work is that there is no map of the battle areas. If used as a stand-alone book, the reader would be easily lost.

The reader leaves this book with a feeling of pain that the women had to endure, either over the losses of their men in the fighting and/or their own travails in prison.

If I were to rate this book among others dealing with women in Ireland's fight for independence, I would rate it third behind McCoole's No Ordinary Women and Ward's Unmanageable Revolutionaries. It does, however, have an extensive bibliography.

Book Review
The Easter Rising
Michael Foy & Brian Barton
Sutton Publishing, Gloucester, 1999
423 pps.

This is a rather straight forward account of the Easter Rising written in 1999, making it the first new survey (until Charles Townshend's 2006 book) in a decade. As it was published well before the release of the witness statements from the military archives, it contains very little which had not already been published in other volumes.

The work is refreshing, however, in that it begins very quickly with the actual events of the Easter Rising. The narrative is site based i.e., it traces the events throughout the week at each individual site. This allows for continuity, but dims events as they relate to one another.

The photographs have all been seen elsewhere, so there is little of interest in that regard. The numerous maps, however, are excellent and offer the reader a real sense of orientation.

There also is a perspective from the British side seldom found in other works on the Easter Rising except by Max Caulfield. The authors have presented a balanced view of events and for that they should be complimented.

The bibliography is not extensive, but it is complete. Any work of a scholarly nature dealing with the events of Easter Week 1916 is listed. The authors have also used official records from both Ireland and England. This book is worthy of one's time.

Book Review
1916: The Easter Rising
Tim Pat Coogan
Cassell & Co., London, 2002
192 pps.

This is a lavishly illustrated book written by one of Ireland's most prolific authors. Tim Pat Coogan has covered all aspects of Irish History in the Twentieth Century.

The main problem one might have with this that although entitled: The Easter Rising, it takes nearly half the book to actually get to Easter Week 1916. The reader could easily become distracted before arriving at the meat of the subject.

Most of the photographs have been previously published in other accounts, but not as many in any one entity. What are very interesting, however, are the copies of the actual written documents and other items which appear. For example, mobilization orders from Thomas MacDonagh, countersigned by Patrick Pearse, battle orders from James Connolly issued on April 25th, and Patrick Pearse's manifesto written from the GPO on April 28th are all fascinating additions to this book.

There are two main maps in the book, one on pages 92-3 which shows the cordoned area of Dublin, and one on pages 96-7 which shows the central area of Dublin between the canals. On the latter map, Richmond Barracks is shown North of the Grand Canal, just West of Clanbrassil Street. This is incorrect as Richmand Barracks was actually West of Dublin off Emmet Road beyond Kilmainham. Errors such as this make the narrative confusing at times.

Coogan offers little in the way of a bibliography. He gives Max Caulfield credit for authorship of the most authoritative work on the Easter Rising, but offers little beyond. This book is nice for the coffee table, but beyond the photos, offers little in the way of scholarly research.

Book Review
Rebels: The Irish Rising of 1916
Peter deRosa
Ballantine Books, New York, 1990
536 pps.

This was the first book which I read dealing with the Easter Rising and I enjoyed it a great deal. It is presented in a chronological fashion, visiting each site daily from beginning to end. It is very fast reading as the style flows well. I would recommend this book as a first step in the study of the events of Easter 1916, although it takes about 240 pages to get to the actual Easter Rising.

In a positive note, the author introduces the prominent players at the outset which greatly assists the novice. On the negative side, there are two maps in the back of the book which are barely adequate. The photographs enhance the reading, but they are the standard period pictures. At the end of the book, there is a section entitled "What Happened Next" which offers a postscript on those who survived and what eventually became of them.

This book offers a generous bibliography. It ends with about one hundred pages describing the aftermath. Much of this deals with the time at Kilmainham and the executions, a topic glossed over in most other accounts.

Book Review
The Easter Rising
Richard Killeen
Thomas Learning, New York, 1995
48 pps.

This is not a very ambitious book, but rather a highly illustrated presentation with numerous photographs and maps. The photos are not new, but the maps are quite good.

One feature of the book which is excellent is the use of timelines for each of the six days of the rising. Sadly, however, it does not extend beyond Saturday, April 29th. The timelines would have been complete had they gone to the executions in May.

There is a very simplistic glossary in the back of the book which explains certain terms and identifies certain buildings in Dublin in 1916. There is also a very basic bibliography.

Consequently, there is very little in this book to be recommended.

Book Review
The Easter Rising: A Guide to Dublin in 1916
Conor Kostick & Lorcan Collins
O'Brien Press, Dublin, 2001
141 pps.

This is a rather unique book in that it owes its origin to "The 1916 Rebellion Walking Tour", organized and operated by the authors. As explained in their introduction, the book is intended to be a companion to the tour, and as such, does not follow the Easter Rising in any chronological/site fashion, but rather along a continuous route covered in one and one half hours.

As such, it presents the Rising in a little different light by forsaking much of the buildup presented in other summaries and focuses upon central Dublin. It does an excellent job in presentation, with good photographs and a good map at the beginning. The only problem with the map is that Richmond Barracks is shown on the South Circular Road near the Grand Canal (noted as Griffith Barracks today) when in fact, Richmond Barracks was on the West side of Dublin, off Emmet Road beyond Kilmainham.

The bibliography is brief, but adequate. I would recommend this book to anyone wishing to gain some insight into the Easter Rising.

There is also a good array of photographs contemporary with events. I would prefer to see a 'then and now' layout, with the insertion of companion photos of the sights as they appear on the walking tour.

Book Review
Agony at Easter
Thomas Coffey
Penguin Books, Baltimore, Maryland, 1971
262 pps.

This is a very readable volume indeed which was published right after the 50th Anniversary of the Easter Rising. As such, it draws almost entirely from Max Caulfield's The Easter Rebellion.

There is little new in the book if one has already read Caulfield, but Coffey decided to frame his work somewhat differently. The entire book centers upon the activities inside the General Post Office (GPO) throughout the week. It is presented in a chronological sequence with very good results. Events which occurred at the Four Courts, South Dublin Union, St. Stephen's Green, Jacob's Biscuit Factory, Boland's Mill and Mount Street Bridge are presented as they are reported to the headquarters in the GPO. This works well except for the events at Mount Street Bridge which is covered in a mere sentence.

The dialogue presented within the GPO has been presented before. One would suspect that most of the direct quotes are from Desmond Fitzgerald, and from those cited in Caulfield. Nevertheless, this is a wonderful chronicle of Easter Week 1916.

Sources are cited at the front of the book and those mentioned are the standards of the time. There are no photographs, but that is not a hindrance as the work reads so well. There are two maps, one of Dublin in 1916, and the other of the GPO area. The maps are quite complete and correct.

This book is of value in researching the Easter Rising. Although Caulfield explores the full scope of events, this does as well, but from a different perspective.

Book Review
The 1916 Rising
Edward Purdon
Mercier Press, Cork, 1999
96 pps.

This very short book is a well written treatment of the Easter Rising, part of Mercier's Compact Irish History Series. The book itself contains very few photographs and a very small map. As with any book in this series, its purpose is not an in-depth study, but rather a well written survey of events.

The first chapter provides the setting for the Easter Rising and also places the event in perspective, both of 1916, and for the history of Ireland in general. The eleven pages of the first chapter are worth the price of the book.

The survey of events in Chapters 3-4 contain enough information to inform, yet not overwhelm the reader. Chapter 5 tells of the executions while the last chapter deals with the aftermath.

The remainder of the book gives a concise biographical index of the individuals of the Rising. This part of the book deals with rebels, the women and the British personalities.

I would recommend this book as a quick introduction to the Easter Rising, as well as other volumes in the series, especially The War of Independence and The Civil War.

Book Review
Rebel Ireland
Sean McMahon
Mercier Press, Cork, 2006
191 pps.

This book is a sham and an utter disappointment! Mercier Press and all of the major booksellers here in the U.S. implied that the work is a new look at the turbulent years from 1916 to 1923. In fact, I was very eager to acquire the book and pre-ordered it through Barnes & Noble prior to its March 2006 release date. I was upset when the bookseller notified me that it had sold out. I later found it available from Irish Books & Media.

As I read the first paragraph, I was immediately struck by the fact that I had already read this work. Upon further inspection, I noticed the fine print on the copyright page which stated "Originally published as three books: The 1916 Easter Rising [1999], The War of Independence [2000], and The Civil War [2001]. I then realized that Mercier Press had merely pressed the three books by 'Edward Purdon' into one with a new cover, with the true author's identity revealed and with a new publication date.

Needless to say, I was most upset. Although the works themselves are quite good, I had already purchased them individually. I consulted a review for the book and apparently the reviewer was unaware of what had been done as well. All I gained for my $20.00 was the fact that the pseudonym Edward Purdon really was Sean McMahon.

Book Review
Easter 1916: The Irish Rebellion
Charles Townshend
Penguin Press, London, 2006
360 pps.

Charles Townshend insists that his book is the first written by a 'historian' dealing with the Easter Rising. He has created an interesting work, one which though thorough, is tedious at certain points.

The author spends time explaining use of the word 'rebellion' in the title, rather than rising. I think that the passage of time has made that distinction less offensive today than it has been in the past. Once, to describe the event as a rebellion would have been 'unionist', while use of the word rising demoted a nationalist. At any rate, the work is the first to use recently released 'witness statements' from Cathal Brugha Barracks as part of the historical research (Annie Ryan's book is a collection of some of the statements, but not a cohesive history of the Easter Rising).

Townshend attempts to dig into the more subjective aspect of the Rising, such as Connolly's decision to join, Pearse's motivation, and the political machinations which were all part of the onset. These are presented well and they do offer insight. This makes the book somewhat different. Instead of being a restatement of events, it is an attempt to sort through the reasons which resulted in those events.

The book contains few photographs, but any student of the Easter Rising would have seen this elsewhere before. The bibliography is excellent.

In summary, this book is not for someone with a casual interest. Nor, can it be read quickly as it does provoke thought. I am not so sure, however, that Townshend does a service by questioning why the particular rebel sites were chosen, for example. Historical fact indicates the rebels' sites, beyond speculating upon the chances for success envisioned by the leaders, what is the point?

Book Review
Where's Where in Dublin
Joseph E.A. Connell, Jnr.
Dublin City, Dublin, 2006
226 pps.

This is an excellent book which goes well beyond the Easter Rising in scope. It is a guide to Dublin for the years 1916- 1923. As such, it offers many intriguing entries.

From the outset, this incredible book is handicapped by its lack of maps. It lists street addresses in alphabetical fashion, but there is no way for the casual tourist to follow events as the only way to use the book would be to stand in front of an address and look into the book to see if it is listed. I consider my knowledge of Dublin during this timeframe to be excellent, but I had to continuously refer to my Ordnance Survey map for orientation.

That being said, the contents of the book are excellent. A person could walk up O'Connell Street from the Liffey and following building to building from the book. The events for each location are described in fine fashion. The book informs, but does not overwhelm.

The appendices in the back of the book are truly outstanding. There is a separate section which contains Michael Collins listings. Also, each military unit of the Volunteers and the Citizen Army are listed by location and the names of the combatants are listed.

I would not hesitate in recommending this book to anyone wishing to follow the trail of the Easter Rising, and the events which followed. It serves both the serious historian and the casual tourist.

Book Review
**Desmond's Rising
Memoirs 1913 to Easter 1916**
Desmond Fitzgerald
Liberties Press, Dublin, 2006
238 pps.

This was originally published in 1966 under the title Memoirs 1913 to Easter 1916. These are the personal recollections of a quasi-major participant who just happened to be posted at the GPO throughout the entire affair.

The author shares his experiences leading up to the Rising as well as the day-to-day occurrences during the week. He also shares with the readers his escape from the GPO and the events which followed the surrender. All of this is presented in a very human way which places the reader in the midst of the events.

This work is much better that Desmond Ryan's The Rising in that it only relates the facts and makes no judgments. It is both humorous and melancholy at the same time assisting the reader in appreciating the vast swing of emotions which must have befallen the participants.

This is real history, presented in a first hand fashion. None of Fitzgerald's recollections have been contested, and nearly all have been quoted by other authors. Next to the articles found in the 1966 Capuchin Annual, I would recommend this book to any student of the Easter Rising wishing to attain a feel for the events.

Book Review
**The Irish Times
Book of the 1916 Rising**
Shane Hegarty & Fintan O'Toole
Gill & Macmillan, Dublin, 2006
216 pps.

A supplement was issued by the *Irish Times* in March 2006 which commemorated the 90th Anniversary of the Easter Rising. This book came from that supplement.

The book itself is quite similar to Tim Pat Coogan's 1916: The Easter Rising in that both works are very graphic in presentation. I prefer this book, however, as it begins immediately with Easter week and moves the reader very quickly through events. It presents the story in a direct manner, making every effort NOT to be judgmental, but to be historically correct. Due to its manner of presentation, a vast assortment of maps is not required.

Most of the photographs have been seen in other accounts, although there are a few that I have not seen.

The real strength of the book lies in its extracts from the Irish Times which appear throughout as a means of drawing the reader back to 1916. Witness statements and other accounts come primarily from Max Caulfield, although oddly, the Capuchin Annual 1966 is not mentioned as a source in the bibliographic list of works.

I think this is a work which has a place in the history of the Easter Rising. I would term is a 'graphic guide' to Easter week rather than a scholarly journey.

The Irish National Anthem: "A Soldier's Song"

The national anthem of Ireland was written by Peadar Kearney and is entitled "A Soldier's Song". Although written in 1907, it was not widely known until it was often sung at the GPO during the Easter Rising.

Peadar Kearney was born at 68 Dorset Street Lower, Dublin, in 1883. He was educated at The Model School and later by the Christian Brothers. He joined the Gaelic League in 1901 and the Irish Republican Brotherhood in 1903. He joined with Patrick Heaney (who composed the music) to create a song which would let Irishmen know that they did not have to join the British Army to become soldiers.

Kearney later gained employment with the Abbey Theatre as a props man and toured England with the company. Kearney left the theatre company in 1916 to take part in the Easter Rising. He was arrested as a rebel and did internment in England.

A Soldier's Song

We'll sing a song, a soldier's song,
With cheering rousing chorus,
As round our blazing fires we throng,
The starry heavens o'er us;
Impatient for the coming fight,
And as we wait the morning's light,
Here in the silence of the night,
We'll chant a soldier's song.

Chorus
**Soldiers are we
whose lives are pledged to Ireland;
Some have come
from a land beyond the wave.
Sworn to be free,
No more our ancient sire land
Shall shelter the despot or the slave.
Tonight we man the gap of danger
In Erin's cause, come woe or weal
'Mid cannons' roar and rifles peal,
We'll chant a soldier's song**

In valley green, on towering crag,
Our fathers fought before us,
And conquered 'neath the same old flag
That's proudly floating o'er us.
We're children of a fighting race,
That never yet has known disgrace,
And as we march, the foe to face,
We'll chant a soldier's song

Chorus

Sons of the Gael! Men of the Pale!
The long watched day is breaking;
The serried ranks of Inisfail
Shall set the Tyrant quaking.
Our camp fires now are burning low;
See in the east a silv'ry glow,
Out yonder waits the Saxon foe,
So chant a soldier's song.

Chorus

Grace Gifford & Joseph Plunkett

The following was taken from:
No Ordinary Women,
Sinead McCoole,
University of Wisconsin, Madison, 2002
p. 64

"Testimonium Status Liberi Ad Matrimonium Proxime Contrahomdum"
(Letter of Freedom to Marry)

Parish Church, Rathmines

"Joseph Plunkett
Kilmainham
Grace Gifford
Rathmines

L. E. Laughlin
3 May, 1916"

The Marriage of Joseph Plunkett & Grace Gifford

Grace Gifford was born on March 4, 1888, in Rathmines, Dublin. She studied art at Dublin Metropolitan School of Art where one of her classmates was Willie Pearse (younger brother of Patrick Pearse). Grace's initiation to the republican cause may have been through her sister, Sidney Gifford Czira, who submitted articles to Arthur Griffith's newspaper, *Sinn Fein*. It was through republican journalism that the Gifford sisters came into contact with Countess Markievicz, Thomas MacDonagh (who married Grace's sister, Muriel), Patrick Pearse and Maud Gonne.

During the Easter Rising, both Thomas MacDonagh and Joseph Plunkett were signatories of the Proclamation. MacDonagh was Commandant of the Volunteer forces at Jacob's Biscuit Factory, while Joseph remained in the GPO.

Joseph Plunkett was the son of Count Plunkett who had received his title for his position as emissary to the Papal Court. Joseph was joined in the Rising by two of his brothers. Joseph and Grace had become engaged in 1915 and the wedding had been set for April 24, 1916. It was to have been a double wedding which included Joseph's sister Geraldine and Thomas Dillon. Concurrent with the advent of the Rising, of which Grace did not know, Joe had surgery on a gland in his neck as a result of tuberculosis and had to leave his hospital bed to join the Rising.

After the surrender, it became quickly apparent that all of the signatories would be shot. Accordingly, Joseph Plunkett was tried and condemned to death by firing squad.

In late afternoon on Wednesday, May 3rd, Grace entered a jeweler's shop in Grafton Street. The owner had put his stock away for the day, but Grace demanded that she be allowed to buy wedding rings, any wedding rings.

From there, she went to Kilmainham Gaol arriving around 6:00PM. Having already secured the appropriate letter of freedom from her church in Rathmines, she was granted permission for the wedding, but she was made to wait until nearly midnight. The actual ceremony took place around 1:30AM in the chapel of the prison. The only light in the chapel was provided by two candles. Two British soldiers acted as witnesses and the quick ceremony was performed by the prison chaplain, Fr. Eugene McCarthy. Upon completion of the marriage, Joseph was immediately returned to his cell, affording the newlyweds no time together.

In her work, Grace Gifford Plunkett, author Marie O'Neill has reproduced the marriage license for Joseph and Grace, which contains the following information:

Registration of Marriage
Joseph Plunkett & Grace Gifford
Issued May 3, 1916

Joseph Plunkett, Full age, bachelor, gentleman, resident Kilmainham Prison
Grace Gifford, Full age, spinster, artist, 29 Oakley Road, Rathmines

"In the presence of Eugene McCarthy, John Smith and John Leacheaky, Sgt., 3rd Br. The Royal Fslrs. Rg."

The Chapel at Kilmainham Gaol

The next, and the last time Joseph and Grace would meet was when Grace was summoned back to the prison a couple of hours later. They were allowed ten minutes together, under the watchful eyes of the guards, in Joseph's cell.

At 3:30AM, Joseph Plunkett was killed by firing squad and Grace Gifford became a widow after a marriage of 3-4 hours. Like all of the leaders of the Easter Rising, Joseph's body was buried in quicklime behind Arbour Hill Prison- neither Joseph's family nor his wife could claim the body. Grace never remarried.

The marriage of these two became one of the most influential events in the immediate change of sentiment towards the Easter Rising. Grace Gifford Plunkett became a committed nationalist, serving time in prison for her activities.

Just after the Easter Rising, Grace suffered not only the loss of her husband, but also that of her brother-in-law, Thomas MacDonagh, her sister Muriel (who drowned leaving two small children) and her father. All of these people left her between May, 1916 and the end of 1917.

Throughout the remainder of her life, Grace became a very successful artist and used those talents to further the Republican cause. She was elected to the Executive of Sinn Fein in 1917, and at the conclusion of the Treaty in 1921, became extremely vocal for the anti-treaty minority.

During the Civil War in 1923, Grace was imprisoned in Kilmainham jail for her anti-treaty activities.

Grace died on December 15, 1955 in Dublin. Her funeral service was officiated by Rev. James Sherwin, the same priest who had brought her into the Roman Catholic Church in 1916. She was buried near the Republican plot in Glasnevin Cemetery.

"Grace"

By Frank & Sean O'Meara (1985)

As we gather in the chapel here in old Kilmainham Jail
I think about these past few weeks, oh will they say we've failed?
From our school days they have told us we must yearn for liberty
Yet all I want in this dark place is to have you here with me

Oh Grace just hold me in your arms and let this moment linger
They'll take me out at dawn and I will die
With all my love I place this wedding ring upon your finger
There won't be time to share our love for we must say goodbye

Now I know it's hard for you my love to ever understand
The love I bare for these brave men, the love for my dear land
But when Pádraic called me to his side down in the GPO
I had to leave my own sick bed, to him I had to go

Oh, Grace just hold me in your arms and let this moment linger
They'll take me out at dawn and I will die
With all my love I'll place this wedding ring upon your finger
There won't be time to share our love for we must say goodbye

Now as the dawn is breaking, my heart is breaking too
On this May morn as I walk out, my thoughts will be of you
And I'll write some words upon the wall so everyone will know
I loved so much that I could see his blood upon the rose.

Oh, Grace just hold me in your arms and let this moment linger
They'll take me out at dawn and I will die
With all my love I'll place this wedding ring upon your finger
There won't be time to share our love for we must say goodbye
For we must say goodbye

Grace Gifford Plunkett
by Philip Naviasky (1918)

Escape from the GPO

By late Friday afternoon, April 28th, the headquarters of the newly proclaimed Republic of Ireland (the GPO) was a burning shambles. The British had brought artillery to bear upon the structure and after two days of shelling, the roof had burned and collapsed. The situation had become so desperate, that the leadership held a meeting to discuss evacuation.

At around 6PM, Patrick Pearse, Sean McDermott, Thomas Clarke, Joseph Plunkett and The O'Rahilly gathered around the bed of James Connolly to plan the evacuation. Their first option was the sewer system, but after finding it impassable, realized that they would have to venture out into the street. It was decided that a strong, safe building was only a full city block away. It was decided that a new headquarters would be established at the Williams & Wood Factory at the corner of Moore Street and Parnell Street. It was also decided that the prisoners would have to be released (as they would surely die if left inside the GPO) and that the women and the wounded would have to be evacuated first. At that time, the Metropole Hotel and the other immediate outposts were evacuated and the men called back to the GPO.. For the women and the wounded, it was decided that they would be taken out of the GPO through tunnels which had been smashed between the buildings down Henry Street to the Coliseum Theatre. This detail was led by Desmond Fitzgerald, George Mahoney and Father Flanagan. When all were ready to leave, James Connolly refused to be taken with the wounded and remained inside the GPO.

The prisoners were released to their own devices which made their exit very hazardous. They did not know the area well, nor had they any idea of a route to safety. They made their way down Henry Street and hid until the Rising had ended.

Previously, The O'Rahilly had led a group of thirty Volunteers out of the GPO in an attempt to reach Parnell Street. They were pinned down in Moore Street and could not advance. Many were either killed or wounded (The O'Rahilly was killed at this time- see *"Death of The O'Rahilly).*

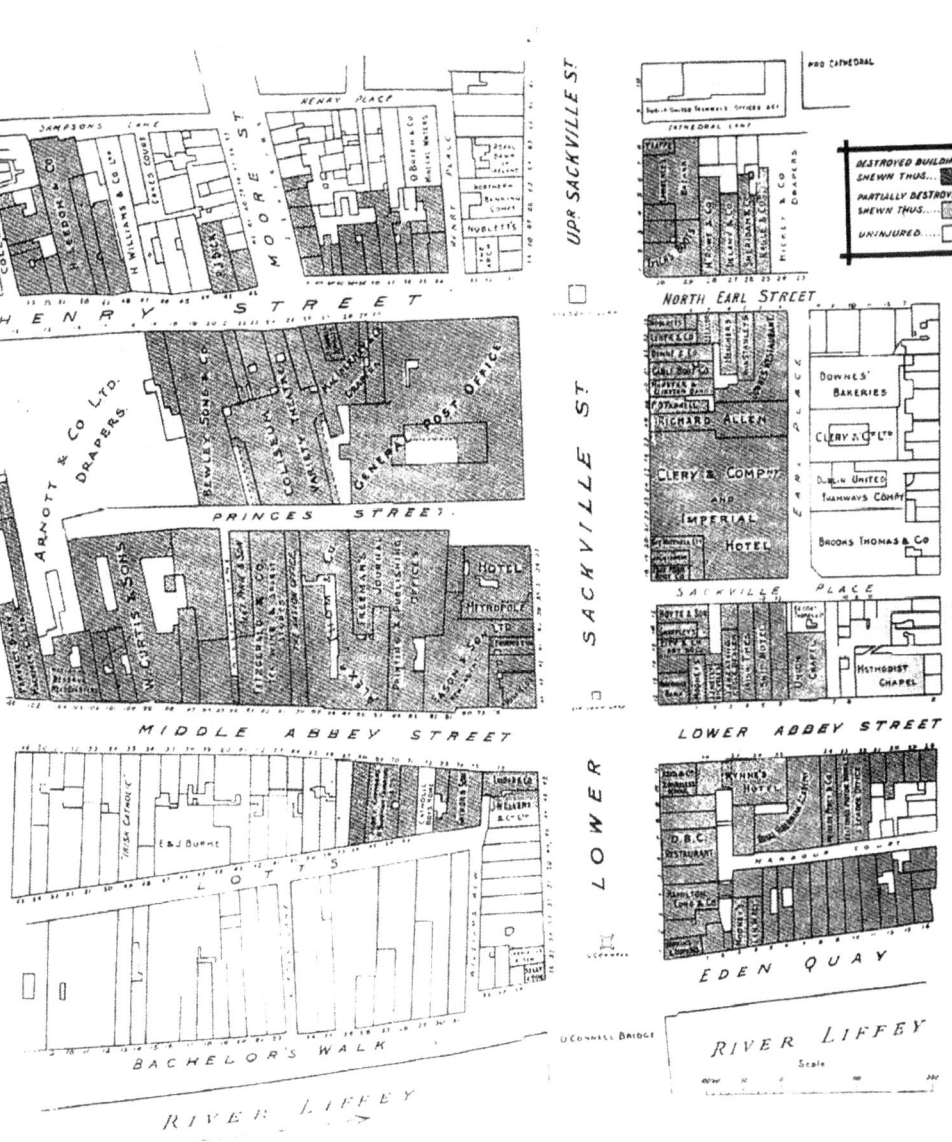

The area around Sackville Street and the GPO

At 8:40PM, Pearse gave the order to evacuate the GPO. The first group left the building by a side door onto Henry Street and moved across to Henry Place. Among the second portion of the garrison were the three women who had refused to evacuate earlier (Elizabeth O'Farrell, Winifred Carney and Julia Grenan) along with James Connolly on a stretcher. Miss Carney carried a note given her by Joseph Plunkett addressed to his fiancée, Grace Gifford.

After the last group had departed the GPO, Pearse again entered the building to ensure that everyone had gone. A short time later, he emerged from the inferno confident that he was the last to leave the GPO. (In his memoirs, Diarmuid Lynch states that Pearse was NOT the last to leave, but that he and Harry Boland had been in the cellar disarming bombs when the building had been evacuated and that they emerged after Pearse had left for the final time.)

In the meantime, the first group of Volunteers had advanced up Henry Place to Moore Lane. At that point, they faced a strong barricade at the corner of Moore Lane and Purnell Street, which prevented them from going up Moore Lane. They then retreated to Henry Place and moved westward along Moore Street. When they had reached the corner, the remnants of The O'Rahilly's group were still in Moore Street facing machineguns. With no other options, the evacuees from the GPO entered a building at the corner which was Cogan's Shop, with a cottage in the rear occupied by the McKane family. During the early hours of Saturday morning, tunneling was done through the buildings on Moore Street. It was decided that the safest place to locate would be in the middle of the block, rather than further up the street to the corner. For that reason, the last headquarters for the Provisional Government of the Republic of Ireland was at Hanlon's Fish Shop, 16 Moore Street. It was from this point that the decision to surrender was made and presented to the British by Nurse O'Farrell on Saturday afternoon..

The plaque marking 16 Moore Street as a historic site.
Unveiled: 2006

The Death of the O'Rahilly

Plaque dedicated to the O'Rahilly in Kerry (1966)

Michael Joseph O'Rahilly was born in Ballylongford, County Kerry on April 22, 1875. He was educated locally and entered the Royal University of Ireland, Dublin to study medicine. He had to drop his studies, however, and return to Kerry to run the family business. Eventually, he married, traveled widely, and spent two different occasions living in the United States. He also had a keen interest in Irish History which led him to Irish nationalism. In his research for his family tree, he discovered that he was the oldest living male, and in the old-time fashion, forever referred to himself as "The O'Rahilly"

He began writing articles for Arthur Griffith's publications, first *United Irishman,* and later *Sinn Fein.* He was the co-founder of the Irish Volunteers in 1913 and personally directed the first major arming of the Volunteers at Howth in 1914.

The O'Rahilly refused membership into the I.R.B. and was not privy to the plans for the Easter Rising. He was in agreement with Eoin MacNeill and Bulmer Hobson that no rising should occur which lacked a chance for success. Immediately before the Easter Rising, Hobson disappeared and the O'Rahilly visited Patrick Pearse, threatening him with a pistol if anything happened to Hobson.

On Saturday, April 22nd, MacNeill published an order in the newspapers which cancelled Volunteer maneuvers which had been planned for the following day. That event would ensure that very few of the men that the I.R.B. had planned for the rising would not muster. The O'Rahilly spent that Saturday night and all day Sunday delivering the order for the stand-down to Cork, Limerick, Kerry and Tipperary.

When he returned to Dublin early Monday morning, he learned that the rising was to commence that morning despite the MacNeill order. He arrived at Liberty Hall in his motorcar (which was used eventually as part of a barricade and destroyed) and presented himself for duty. He delivered his famous line: "Because I helped wind the clock I came to hear it strike".

The O'Rahilly spent the entire week in the GPO, mainly on the upper floor away from the leaders. There existed some tension between he and them and most of his time was spent directing the Volunteers on the roof, and caring for the prisoners. Much of his activity has been recorded by Desmond Fitzgerald's Memoirs 1913-1916.

By Friday, April 28th, the GPO had been badly damaged by fire and was still ablaze. The O'Rahilly volunteered to lead a party of rebels in search of a route to the Williams and Wood building at the corner of Parnell and Moore Streets. That destination was where the leadership had hoped to establish a new headquarters.

The group made its way from the GPO using the Henry Street exit and moved to the West to the corner of Moore Street. At that point, they were devastated by machineguns firing from a barricade up the street at its junction with Parnell Street. Although seriously wounded, The O'Rahilly, slumped in a doorway on Moore Street, gathered enough strength to cross Moore Street and find shelter at the corner of Sackville Lane. His run across Moore Street exposed him and he received more wounds.

Sometime after dark on Friday evening and Saturday afternoon, The O'Rahilly died at that location. It is certain that he lived for sometime after arriving at that place, for he accomplished some very remarkable things. One thing is for certain, due to the heavy fire down Moore Street, no one could reach him to offer aid or protection.

Before he died, he dipped his finger in his own blood and wrote his name on the doorway beside his head. He also took a note from his pocket which was written to him by his son while he had been in the GPO. On the back of this note he wrote his last message to his wife which read: "Written after I was shot. Darling Nancy I was shot leading a rush up Moore Street and took refuge in a doorway. While I was there I heard the men pointing out where I was and made a bolt for the laneway I am in now. I got more than one bullet I think. Tons and tons of love dearie to you and the boys and to Nell and Anna. It was a good fight anyhow. Please deliver this to Nannie O'Rahilly, 40 Herbert Park, Dublin. Good-Bye Darling". The piece of paper that he had used had a bullet hole in it when it was found.

The O'Rahilly's son, Aodogan, has written a biography of his father entitled: <u>Winding the Clock- O'Rahilly and the 1916 Rising</u>. Also, on Friday, April 29, 2005, artist Shane Cullen unveiled a sculpture commemorating The O'Rahilly at the spot he died. The letter he wrote to his wife was reproduced on the plaque.

The name of Sackville Place was also changed to O'Rahilly Parade.

The Role of the Capuchin Friars

In the Easter Rising

Sources: The Capuchin Annual 1966
An Phoblacht "Patriot Priest" 1 May 1997
Capuchin Archives, Church Street, Dublin, "Echoes of the Rising's Final Shots"

Throughout the Easter Rising, representatives of the Catholic Church played very important roles. Among those who came to the forefront were the Capuchin Friars of Church Street. Because of the location of the friary, they were thrust into the fray from the beginning.

The main players were Fathers Albert, Augustine, Aloysius and Sebastian. The recently released document, "Echoes of the Rising's Final Shots" also lists the activities of Fr. Columbus Murphy, but those activities mirror perfectly the activities of Fr. Albert in The Capuchin Annual 1966. Were they the same person?

Cathal O'Shannon receiving a visit from Fr. Augustine OFM Cap.

According to Fr. Albert, the first indication that something was amiss occurred around 12:30PM on Monday after, April 24th. At that time, a youngster had been shot in Church Street and was brought into Father Matthew Hall. Going to investigate events outside, Fr. Albert noted that rebel barricades had already appeared at both ends of Church Street by 1:30PM. Shooting continued throughout the day and into the night.

On Tuesday morning, Frs. Albert, Jarlath and Sebastian had been recruited to assist with the wounded and displaced at both Richmond Hospital and the North Dublin Union. By late Tuesday afternoon, Father Matthew Hall in Church Street had been taken over by the rebels as a hospital and was being staffed by members of Cumann na mBan.

Fr. Albert OFM Cap.

Wednesday saw the houses on Church Street occupied by the rebels and the entire area fortified. Work continued in Father Matthew Hall as casualties began to mount. Late into the evening and all day Thursday, the bloody battle for North King Street raged and the pressure for medical services in the hall were stretched to the limit. The intensity continued to increase both Friday and into Saturday morning with dead and wounded numbers growing as the hours passed.

By early Saturday afternoon, many of the wounded in Father Matthew Hall were critical and required movement to hospital for any chance of survival. Because of that, Fathers Aloysius and Augustine went into Church Street under cover of a white flag in order to meet with the British and arrange a truce to remove the wounded. They were taken to different levels of authority before finally being told that a surrender had been arranged by Patrick Pearse and that hostilities were in fact finished. As the Four Courts garrison, which had authority for Church Street, did not believe the surrender story, a truce was arranged for the area until a handwritten note from Pearse could be obtained by the priests. Accordingly, on Sunday morning, the two Capuchin Friars traveled to Dublin Castle to arrange permission to visit Pearse.

While at the Castle, it was suggested to them that because James Connolly was a prisoner/patient there in the Castle, they should also encourage him to sign a similar surrender note in case some of the rebels in Church Street were members of the Citizen Army and not Volunteers. That being done, the two men were taken to Arbour Hill Prison and met with Patrick Pearse. He gladly wrote another surrender note for them and conveyed to them his sadness over the death and destruction caused by the Rising.

As the notes were enough to convince Commandant Daly to surrender the Four Courts garrison, the two priests were asked to perform the same task at the Jacob's Biscuit Factory. They agreed and were taken there where they met with a bellicose John MacBride and his superior Commanadnt MacDonagh. Along with Thomas MacDonagh, the Capuchins were taken to the South Dublin Union to convince Commandant Ceannt to obey the surrender order. Having acoomplished that mission, the two priests accompanied MacDonagh to his actual surrender to the British. Upon the surrender of these forces, the rebels were forced to march into captivity. All of these surrenders had been accomplished through the efforts of the Capuchin Friars.

Father Matthew Hall, Church Street, Dublin

On Monday, May 1st, a message was received at the Church Street Friary that James Connolly wished to see Father Aloysius. The priest went and spent time with the Citizen Army Commandant. Connolly offered praise for the role of priests during the Rising, quite a statement from a true socialist.

On Tuesday, Father Aloysius administered communion to James Connolly. That evening, the priest was summoned to Kilmainham Gaol to administer the needs of Patrick Pearse, Thomas MacDonagh and Thomas Clarke. Early the next morning, he was told to leave; he protested that he could not complete his duties in not allowed to stay, but he was required to leave anyway. Interestingly, Pearse had been given a crucifix by Father Aloysius at their first meeting and when Pearse returned it to the priest, he had carved "P.M.P" on the back. Another account says that Father Augustine was with Father Aloysius throughout that Tuesday night/ Wednesday morning.

On Wednesday evening, the priests were again summoned to Kilmainham, and on this occasion four of them went as there were four prisoners to be executed. On this and all subsequent visits, the priests were allowed to stay through the executions. The priests were Fathers Albert, Aloysius, Augustine and Sebastian. This activity continued through to the following Monday when the last of the fourteen (McDermott and Connolly) were executed.

The significance of the Capuchin Friars during the Easter Rising cannot be underestimated. In essence, they gave comfort to the wounded, administered to the dying, arranged the truce and eventual surrender, and left a record of the final hours of those executed.

The Capuchin Friary
Church Street, Dublin

James Connolly as Military Commander

Much has been made of the role of James Connolly in the Easter Rising with respect to his tenacity and courage as head of the ITGWU. Also, his heroic death at the hands of the firing squad while bound to a chair has been added to Irish folklore. It is my opinion, however, that his greatest gift to the Easter Rising was his role as military commander.

In 1882, at the age of fourteen, Connolly joined the British Army, and remained for seven years, all based in Ireland. It was during this time that two things occurred: (1) He received military training from his future enemy and knew well their ways, and (2) He witnessed first had the terrible treatment of the Irish people through the brutality of the British. The latter lesson stayed with him forever in the form of intense hatred for the British Army. As head of the ITGWU, Connolly's experience during the Lockout of 1913 convinced him that the workers would need armed protection in case of any future incidents. For that reason, he founded the Citizen Army, a small, but extremely well trained military force. It was his desire that it would be utilized in any rising against the British in the city of Dublin. Because of that reasoning, he revolutionized urban tactics and trained the Citizen Army in his methods.

James Connolly fully analyzed urban warfare and established two maxims used during the Easter Rising. First, England was a capitalist country and therefore would not destroy capital investments in quelling a disturbance. That meant, the defenders against the British would not have to worry about facing artillery. Secondly, the city of Dublin lended itself extremely well to urban warfare with its narrow streets. Defensive positions could be easily held by a few well trained men.

Fundamental to defensive fortification according to Connolly were loop holing, tunneling and barricades. The loop holing gave the defenders excellent protection during an assault upon them, and also offered excellent fields of fire for them. Tunnels were to be cut from building to building which would allow the movement of personnel down a full street without detection. The barricades could be used as defensive barriers whether manned or not.

For the Easter Rising, the selection of the main rebel garrisons was done by Thomas MacDonagh and Joseph Plunkett as Connolly's forces were only admitted to the plans in the late stages. The primary purpose of the positions eventually manned was to interdict the flow of British forces from the various points of entry into the city as well movements from the various barracks.

When the Headquarters Battalion seized the GPO, Connolly assumed command of the garrison and its environs. He dictated the positions to be taken and the defenses constructed within the posts. He directed fortification of the GPO and during its initial taste of battle on Monday against the British lancers on Sackville Street, it was Connolly who insisted upon restraint until the most favorable time to attack occurred. Unfortunately, some of the rebels on the roof were premature and although lancers were killed, the effect could have been much more devastating had they fully complied with their orders.

Upon leaving Liberty Hall to take the GPO, Connolly was asked his opinion of the coming battle and his response was 'we will all be slaughtered'. Regardless, he continued with courage and steadiness.

As the week progressed, he constantly altered his military dispositions in response to the British. He often left the GPO going into the adjacent streets and checking the strength of his defenses. He physically checked existing barricades for strength and often challenged his troops regarding the preparation of their positions. It was during his time in the streets that he was wounded twice on Thursday. The first injury occurred while checking a barricade. Connolly was an incredible example to his men as he demonstrated no fear, even when the bullets began to fly. While at the barricade, he excused himself from the position commander saying that he was wanted back at the GPO. Upon entering the building, he surreptitiously asked the medical officer to join him behind a curtain where he exposed his arm and asked that his wound be dressed. He then swore the man to secrecy concerning the event and returned to checking his defenses.

The next venture that took him into the street was to lead a small detail of men to fortify a new position. After he had placed his men, he was returning to the GPO when he was hit in the ankle by a bullet ricochet off the pavement. He bullet had shattered his ankle and he had to crawl back towards the GPO before he was found and was carried back to his headquarters. That wound was extremely serious, and due to the lack of proper medical supplies, and Connolly's refusal to be taken to hospital, he was to suffer incredible pain over the next two days.

He was placed upon a stretcher in the GPO and would endure periods of unconsciousness. During those times, military matters were assumed by The O'Rahilly, but as soon as Connolly awoke, he would again assume his role. By Friday, he had himself placed upon a mobile stretcher and ordered himself rolled from point to point within the GPO to insure that the defenses were to his liking.

To exemplify the importance of James Connolly's military stature within the GPO command structure, the two most important decisions made after Monday were only made with his assent. The leaders gathered around his stretcher in the GPO to consult with him about evacuation of the building on Friday. They also suggested to him that he be evacuated with the wounded to hospital, but he emphatically declined. The second decision was reached on Moore Street on Saturday when again they gathered around a bed where he lay to discuss surrender. Neither of these decisions would have been made without his agreement.

After Pearse had agreed with unconditional surrender, he too prepared notes for his various Citizen Army garrisons ordering them to surrender. The point being that not all of the rebels would have surrendered solely upon Pearse's order.

James Connolly

Liberty Hall

Cathal Brugha at South Dublin Union

On Thursday, April 27th, one of the most courageous and outstanding feats of human endeavor occurred in the Easter Rising. It happened at the South Dublin Union and would place one person forever in the annals of Irish History.

Cathal Brugha was second in command of the Garrison to Eamonn Ceannt. At around 4:00PM, he led a group of Volunteers occupying the Nurse's Home. The opposing British had reinforced their assault units to the point that fifty experienced soldiers from Portobello Barracks had been added. As those forces entered the Nurse's Home, Ceannt gave the order for the James Street garrison to withdraw in order to assist Brugha at his position. The order was misinterpreted and the forces in the Nurse's Home withdrew instead. In essence, two garrisons withdrew from their posts leaving one unattended and Cathal Brugha alone to withstand the assault.

He had hidden behind a hallway barricade and encountered the British upon their entry. He fought them off despite the fact that they used grenades as well as rifles. During the fight, he was wounded by both bullets and shrapnel. Despite his wounds, he was able to extricate himself and crawl into a small yard in the rear of the building. From that position, he was able to see both the doors and the hallway which passed through the kitchen.

He had with him an automatic pistol and he positioned himself on the ground, propped up against a wall. During his time there, he did not allow the British to advance. Because of all of the rifle shots, Ceannt and the rebels with him were certain that Brugha had been killed.

As Ceannt believed that the way was clear for the British to advance upon his position and eliminate his force, he gathered his men, thanked them for their service and prayed with them. But the assault did not materialize. From a distance, they could hear a very weak voice singing:

"God save Ireland, say we proudly.
God save Ireland, we say all,
Whether on scaffold high
Or the battlefield we die."

The voice, of course, was that of Cathal Brugha. Ceannt sent a scout to see what had occurred. He came upon Brugha, his gun ready, sitting in an ever-widening arc of his own blood. He would pause occasionally from his singing and fire a round towards the building. He would then call out a challenge to the British. By then, unknown to him, the British had left. He had held off the entire force for over two hours and had saved the position as well as Eamonn Ceannt and about forty Volunteers.

Ceannt rushed to Brugha in the yard and knelt beside him. As Ceannt had tears in his eyes, Brugha asked his comrades to sing "God Save Ireland" with him. He then collapsed from loss of blood and exhaustion.

As a result of the action, Brugha had sustained over **twenty five** wounds, some of which included severed arteries. He was taken to Union Hospital. Ceannt was certain that Cathal Brugha would die.

In fact, after the surrender, the British did not even arrest him. His condition was so grave that they never expected him to live, let alone recover. He did recover, of course, and played a major role in the War for Independence (1919-1921). He served as Minister of Defense during that period.

Later, he took the Republican side during the Irish Civil War (1922) and was eventually killed on the streets of Dublin. He was barricaded in a hotel on Sackville Street with other Republicans when the Free State soldiers assaulted the position. The others in his group surrendered, but he refused. He emerged from the building firing his weapons and was shot down. He died a couple of days later.

The Murder of Francis Sheehy-Skeffington

Francis Sheehy-Skeffington was a relative non-player in the Easter Rising who became the eternal innocent victim. His only role was as a pacifist trying to prevent looting on Sackville Street. He had, however, gained a reputation as a feminist as well as a pacifist making him well known to the British.

Skeff (as he was called) had been on the Dublin political scene as early as 1905 when he joined the United Irish League. During the 1913 Lockout, he was a member of the Peace Committee and tried to use negotiations as a means of breaking the deadlock. He was also vice-chairman of the Citizen Army upon its formation, only agreeing to serve if it were used in a strictly defensive posture. He left the Citizen Army when it began training for offensive use.

After trying to halt the looting on Sackville Street on Monday, April 24th, Skeff was walking home around 7:30PM when he was arrested at Portobello Bridge. As his activities (and those of his wife, Hanna, who was a militant suffragette) regarding the fight against conscription, and formation of an Irish republic were well-known, he was held by the British at Portobello Barracks.

A British Officer, Captain Bowen-Colthurst, took possession of Skeffington to whom he referred as 'the Sinn Fein prisoner'. That evening, Bowen-Colthurst took Skeffy with his force on a raid, using the prisoner as a human shield. During the foray, Bowen-Colthurst shot a boy in cold blood. Later, the party captured two journalists, and returned to Portobello Barracks.

The next morning, Tuesday, April 25th, Bowen-Colthurst went to the guardhouse demanding that the three prisoners be put into his custody. That was done and around 10:30AM, the Captain ordered them all shot by a makeshift firing squad. They were all shot in the back. Bowen-Clothurst reported that the prisoners were shot trying to escape.

The matter may have never become public if it were not for a British officer who reported the events as 'repulsive'.

After the Easter Rising, Bowen-Clothurst faced court martial for the three murders. He was found guilty, but insane, and incarcerated in Broadmoor Asylum for twenty months. Later he emigrated to British Columbia, Canada, where he lived on pension until he died in 1966.

Skeff's widow, Hanna Sheehy-Skeffington testified at trial and was offered compensation by the British government. She refused any money as she felt that would dishonor the memory of her husband. She remained an active Republican for the rest of her life.

Hanna Sheehy-Skeffington

Hanna and Margaret Pearse-
Mother of Patrick & Willie

Sir Roger Casement

Roger Casement was born September 1, 1864, in Sandycove, near Dublin. He was raised as a Protestant although his mother had him secretly baptized Catholic. By the time he was ten years old, both his parents had died and he was raised in Ulster by his father's relatives.

At age nineteen, he was working in Belgian Africa. In 1892, Casement joined the British Colonial Office and for the next decade, he endeavored to expose mistreatment of the natives and their exploitation through the forced labor system. His expose` about Belgian abuses led to knighthood in 1911. He resigned from colonial service in 1912.

In 1913, Sir Roger joined the Irish Volunteers. Casement was totally dedicated to Irish nationalism and he reasoned that the First World War was a perfect time to enlist German assistance toward that end. In 1914, he sailed to Germany via America. He conducted himself in the form of an Irish 'diplomat'. His mission to Germany was two-fold: (1) He wished to enlist material aid in the form of weapons and German officers to assist Irish rebels at the time of a rising, and (2) He also wanted to create an Irish Brigade from among prisoners held by the Germans who were Irish. It was his intention to use this unit in Ireland to assist in the event of a rising.

Casement was unsuccessful in his attempt to raise an Irish Brigade as the prisoners would not enroll. He did, however, manage to get the Germans to send arms to Ireland. They were carried aboard the ship *Aud* which managed to evade the British blockade and arrive at Tralee Bay just before the rising. For various reasons, the arms were lost.

Sir Roger, meanwhile left Germany soon after the *Aud* and sailed aboard a submarine, the *U-19*. Casement wished to get to Ireland to stop any rising as he was certain it was premature and doomed to failure. He landed at Banna Strand on April 21st, but was captured almost immediately. His two companions, Monteith and Bailey were able to avoid capture, so Sir Roger was alone at the time he was apprehended.

Once identified by the British, he was charged with treason, sabotage and espionage. After a highly publicized trial, he was stripped of his knighthood and sentenced to death.

After the horrors of the May executions in Dublin, there was a concerted effort to save Sir Roger. During the period of appeal, a 'diary' was found and distributed by the British which besmirched his reputation as it painted him as a latent homosexual. These allegations cooled any thought of clemency and he was hanged at Pentonville Prison on August 3rd. Casement's body was quickly buried in quicklime at the prison.

In the 1960's, the body was repatriated and returned to Ireland where it was buried with full military honors in the Republican Plot at Glasnevin Cemetery.

Ironically, he was received into the Catholic Church immediately before his hanging. He did not know that he had been baptized as a baby.

The Spirituality of the Rebel Leaders
Source: The Catholic Standard April 29, 1966
Interview with Rev. Fr. Leonard Coughlan OFM Cap.
April 4, 2004

It seems that too often the leaders of the Easter Rising are seen as naïve idealists who sacrificed their lives knowingly for the freedom of Ireland. While that may be true, there certainly was more substance to those men than idealism. Considerable evidence exists which suggests a great spiritual depth to those men as they prepared for the inevitable. It must be emphasized that the spirituality included James Connolly as much as the others.

During the late hours of May 3rd, two priests from the Capuchin Friary on Church Street, Father Aloysius and Father Augustine were summoned to Kilmainham Gaol to administer the final sacraments to Thomas Clarke, Patrick Pearse and Thomas MacDonagh. The reason these particular priests were summoned was that they had insured the surrender to halt the Easter Rising during the previous week by visiting Patrick Pearse at Arbour Hill Prison and delivering his handwritten surrender note the various garrisons. It was during that visit that Father Aloysius had left a crucifix with Pearse.

As Father Aloysius approached Pearse's cell in Kilmainham, he looked through the spy hole. "Pearse was there kneeling and the light showing on his face as he clasped the crucifix". The crucifix was returned to Father Aloysius with the initials P.M.P. carved into the back. (Upon inquiring at the Capuchin Friary in 2004, the author was informed that the crucifix was given to the Pearse family).

The two priests were not allowed to stay with the condemned until their execution and they were forced to leave Kilmainham. They did so under protest. Subsequent to this, and because of their unusually strong protest, priests were allowed to stay with the prisoners through their executions.

Father Leonard has related other stories. Michael Mallin's spiritual bearing was so strong that it led to the conversion of Countess Markievicz. Mallin's wife visited him at Kilmainham just prior to his execution and brought their children with her. One of them was a daughter named Una, aged 6. Mallin had written for his wife the following: "I would like you to dedicate Una to the service of God and St. Joseph. Una did, in fact, become a nun and was Mother Delores, a Loreto Sister. Two of Mallin's sons became Jesuit priests.

Sean MacDermott was a deeply religious man despite what has been written to the contrary. His last writings to his brothers and sisters included the following: "By the time this reaches you, I will, with God's mercy, have joined in heaven my father and mother as well as my dear friends who have been shot during the week. I have priests with me almost constantly in the past twenty four hours."

Father Albert, OFM Cap., also from the Church Street Friary, ministered to the condemned prisoners. He has left a wonderful description of the last hours of Sean Heuston.

Having been summoned to Kilmainham on Sunday night, May 7th, Father Albert along with Father Augustine hastened to the jail. Father Albert first went to Michael Mallin's cell and Father Augustine ministered to Eamonn Ceannt. Fr. Albert then went to Sean Heuston's cell where he found him kneeling in prayer. Because the only candle in the cell had burned out, the two of them prayed together in darkness. It was Father Albert's statement that Heuston was not afraid to die, in fact he was looking forward to soon meeting again with Patrick Pearse and the other leaders. The priest and the prisoners continued praying even after the small piece of white paper had been pinned over his heart for the firing squad. Father Albert's final statement was: "Never before did I realize that a man could fight so bravely, and die so beautifully and so fearlessly as did the heroes of Easter Week. On the morning of Sean Heuston's death, I would have given the world to have been in his place; he died in such a noble and sacred cause and went forth to meet...."

This brings us to James Connolly, the hardened socialist. In a political sense, socialism in its purist form leaves little or no room for religion. James Connolly certainly subscribed to socialism in the fullest extent. Father Aloysius, however, has left us with an account of the final days of James Connolly and his spiritual temperament.

It was Connolly who requested to see Father Aloysius. The priest had to promise the British that he was only seeing the prisoner in his capacity as a priest. They had feared that Connolly might use the priest as a messenger. Father Aloysius relayed this information to Connolly and the prisoner's reply was: "It is as a priest that I want to see you. I have seen and heard of the brave conduct of priests and nuns during the week and I believe that they are the best friends of the workers".

On the morning of May 12th, Father Aloysius was summoned to Dublin Castle to see James Connolly. He heard his confession and gave him Holy Communion. After that, he rode in the ambulance which transported him to Kilmainham for his execution. The priest stayed with him until he was executed, a task accomplished by strapping him to a chair as his wounds prevented him from standing.

The testaments left behind by the Capuchin priests, and others presented by Father Leonard Coughlan give a very strong spiritual being to the leaders of the Easter Rising in the last days of their lives. Each and every one of them utilized the religious sacraments available to them prior to their deaths. Their faith in Ireland was only surpassed by their Catholic faith in God.

Father Leonard Coughlan with the crucifix given/returned from Patrick Pearse

Audio Tapes: Fr. Leonard Coughlan OFM Cap.
"Memories of Easter Week 1916"
"Rebirth of a Nation"
"Poems of the 1916 Leaders"

Upon a visit to the Capuchin Friary on Church Street in Dublin in 2004, I was introduced to Fr. Leonard Coughlan, OFM Cap. At that time, he was 92 years old and very eager to talk about the Easter Rising.

I told him that I was very familiar with the role of the Capuchon Friars (Frs. Albert, Augustine, Aloysius and Sebastian) throughout the Rising and their activities through the executions phase. He delighted me with his memories of those Friars and offered me the audio tapes.

It is worthwhile to note that the Friary and the building directly north (the former Father Matthew Hall) have an incredible aura of the Rising about them. The St. Mary's of the Angels Church, on the south side of these two buildings was also involved throughout the turbulent period 1916- 1923. Parts of the altar of the church were in fact carved by Patrick Pearse's father.

Regarding the tapes, "Rebirth of a Nation" is oral history offered by Fr. Leonard based upon notes and stories passed along to him by the above mentioned Friars. These offer an unusually rare insight into the faith and motivation of the leaders of 1916 as well as the depth of their spirit.

The tape also relates the demeanor of those men in the last days and hours before their executions.

"Memories of Easter Week 1916" is a truly moving oral history of the leaders during the first week of May and up to their executions. The presentation imparts the spirituality demonstrated by all of the condemned. Their faith in both their actions and in their religion come bursting forth in the words.

"Poems of the 1916 Leaders" offers the listener an opportunity to explore the soul of each of the men included and to more fully understand their commitment to Ireland and to God. Each time this tape is played, something very new is felt, as there is so much depth to what these men left in the written word.

I am so thankful for the opportunity to have met and spoken to Fr. Leonard. He was most gracious in his time with me and he is truly my personal link to 1916.

Cumann na mBan
and the Role of Women in the Easter Rising

In 1913, when the Irish Volunteers were formed, a group of women met in Wynn's Hotel in Dublin to discuss the formation of a woman's organization which would work in conjunction, yet independently of the Volunteers. On April 4, 1914, the organization was officially launched by Countess Markievicz, Agnes O'Farrell, Jennie Wyse-Power and Louise Gavan Duffy. It was named *Cumann na mBan* (League of Women).

Its mandate was to advance the cause of Irish liberty and to train member in first aid, drill and rifle practice. Explicitly, the group was to aid the men of Ireland.

At the outset of the Easter Rising, Cumann na mBan was integrated with the Irish Volunteers and the Citizen Army into the Army of the Irish Republic. It should be noted that there were female members of the Citizen Army as James Connolly had always expounded equality between men and women.

On Easter Monday, over 40 Cumann na mBan members entered the GPO, and by nightfall, women were established in all of the rebel garrisons except one. Eamonn daValera had barred them from the Boland's garrison, a very serious mistake as later on they could have performed duties which had to be done by men.

The women in the garrisons did all types of chores. They performed the traditional duties of food preparation, nursing, and reloading weapons. They also performed many non-traditional duties such as the transfer of arms and ammunition between locations, courier service under fire and scouting expeditions.

Many of them joined the combat. Countess Markievicz shot a policeman near St. Stephen's Green and is reputed to have sniped a British soldier from the Royal College of Surgeons. Some women were killed during the fighting including Margueretta Keogh, shot at South Dublin Union.

At Father Matthew Hall on Church Street, the Cumann na mBan women had established a hospital. When it came time to evacuate, the women helped move the casualties to Richmond Hospital under fire. They remained at the Capuchin Church that evening and dispersed with those attending Mass the following morning.

At the time of the surrender, Patrick Pearse asked a Cumann na mBan member, Elizabeth O'Farrell to act as his emissary to the British. She risked her life continuously Friday and Saturday carrying Pearse's surrender order to all of the garrisons.

In the end, over 70 women were arrested by the British as insurgents. Twelve remained in custody beyond May, 1916. After the Rising, most of the women remained true to the Republicanism and during the Civil War, took the anti-treaty side. Many of them, including Countess Markievicz and Maud Gonne MacBride spent numerous stints in prison due to their activities.

Maud Gonne MacBride

A Short Biography of the Countess

Countess Markievicz played a very active and significant role in the Easter Rising and because of it, was sentenced to death at her court martial.

She was born in London in 1868 as Constance Georgina Gore-Booth. The family held a huge estate at Lissadell in County Sligo and that was where she was raised. Having been born into wealth and leisure, she decided to study art and went off to London in 1893. By 1898, she had moved on to study in Paris where she met Count Casimir Markievicz. They eventually married in 1901 and they returned to Ireland to live. The marriage did not last and after the birth of their daughter, they separated and he returned to his native Ukraine.

In 1906, the Countess rented a small cottage on the County Dublin shore where she encountered the newspaper, *Sinn Fein*, left behind from the previous renter. She found that she agreed with the idea of Irish independence from British rule, and from that point forward was a committed nationalist.

By 1908, she had joined both the Sinn Fein political party and *Inghinidhe na hEerann* (Daughters of Ireland). In 1909, she founded *Fianna Eireann*, a boy scout-type organization which included military drill.

In the 1913 Lockout, the Countess worked in a soup kitchen and forged an eternal bond with the poor of Dublin. Later in life, she would dispossess herself and contribute anything she had to the poor.

By 1915, she had joined James Connolly's Citizen Army, an organization which offered full equality for women. As such, she was placed second in command to Commandant Mallin at the St. Stephen's Green garrison during the Rising. She shouldered a weapon on numerous occasions during the week and is reputed to have killed a couple of men.

Upon the surrender, the garrison was formed up in front of the Royal College of Surgeons and was marched into captivity with Commandant Mallin and the Countess at the head. She was arrested and was the only woman held in solitary confinement at Kilmainham Gaol.

At her court martial, she pled guilty to the charges with the statement "I did what was right and I stand by it." She was sentenced to death, but her sentence was commuted because of her sex.

Surrender of the Countess

Return of the Countess from Prison 1917

The Countess was finally released from prison in 1917, but by 1918, she was back in jail for anti-British activities. While in prison, she was elected a Member of Parliament as a Sinn Fein candidate. She was, therefore, the first woman MP, but she refused her seat in that body as she would never swear allegiance to the King of England.

She fought for independence during the Anglo-Irish War, but was firmly on the anti-treaty side during the Irish Civil War.

In 1926, the Countess joined the *Fianna Fail*, the new political party led by Eamonn deValera. She was made a cabinet member of the new government, but never took her seat as she died soon afterward.

Over 250,000 people lined the streets for her funeral procession in Dublin. She was buried in the Republican Plot at Glasnevin Cemetery and her eulogy was read by Eamonn deValera.

The Battle for Mount Street Bridge
Wednesday, April 26, 1916

In preparation for the Easter Rising, the Military Council of the I.R.B. planned to occupy locations which would most impede the British Army from subduing the rebel headquarters located in the GPO on Sackville Street. Toward that end, sites were selected which would restrict movement from the various military barracks, from the city train stations and from the main port of embarkation into Dublin, Kingstown.

To secure the route from Kingstown, Commandant deValera sent an unusually small force of 13 Volunteers under the command of Lt. Malone into the Ballsbridge neighborhood with the mandate not to allow British reinforcements to reach the city center. The reason that the location received so few troops was due to the very low turnout on Easter Monday.

Lt. Malone selected four locations to be occupied: Carisbrook House at the fork of Northumberland and Shelbourne Roads, No. 25 Northumberland Road, St. Stephen's Parochial School and its adjacent hall, and Clanwilliam House on the north side of Mount Street Bridge. Carisbrook House was quickly abandoned as Malone soon realized that he would receive no reinforcements and he had inadequate manpower to hold the site.

The disposition of troops was as follows: seven Volunteers in Clanwilliam House, four at the parochial school, and just two at No. 25 Northumberland Road. Early in the day, the men set about fortifying their positions.

Around 9:30AM on Wednesday, Lt. Malone received a message from James Connolly stating that about 2000 British troops had been landed at Kingstown and would be approaching his position in the next few hours.

At about 12:30PM, the leading edge of the British force made the turn onto Northumberland Road. Its orders were to proceed *directly* to Trinity College. To that end, the first formation, Sherwood Foresters, entered into a tremendous crossfire. The British troops were little more than raw recruits and were stunned by the fire from No. 25 Northumberland by Lt. Malone and James Grace. What they failed to understand at the time was that they were being fired upon by all three locations. After about two hours, the British succeeded in quieting No. 25, killing Lt. Malone in the process. James Grace was able to elude capture within the house and escaped later.

In keeping with their orders, the British continued towards Mount Street Bridge, suffering horrible casualties in the process. There was never any thought on the part of the British to bypass that bridge for another. They did, however, decide to try and outflank the positions by going up both Percy Place and Percy Lane. That tactic proved equally disastrous as the Eleven remaining Volunteers continued to riddle them with bullets.

Next, snipers were sent to the bell tower of St. Mary's Church on Haddington Road with the idea of finishing the shooters in Clanwilliam House. They were unsuccessful. Meanwhile, George Reynolds and his force in Clanwilliam House continued to withstand the British with effective fire. They were beginning to realize that there would be no help coming from deValera around the corner at Boland's Bakery and that they were on their own.

On numerous occasions between 2:30 and 7:00PM when the fight ended, shooting was suspended so that bodies could be removed from Mount Street Bridge. This practice was initially started by a teenage girl who bravely walked onto the bridge through all of the shooting to assist a wounded soldier. Gradually, the fighting would begin again, the bridge would fill with dead and wounded, and then hostilities would cease to evacuate the wounded.

At 6:00PM, the British received reinforcements from Kingstown and eliminated the four man garrison at the school. As the Volunteers evacuated that position, Joe Clark was captured by the British, but the other three escaped.

By 7:00PM, Clanwilliam House was fully ablaze, but four of the Volunteers were able to escape. George Reynolds, Richard Murphy and Patrick Doyle perished in the flames, although all three were dead from gunfire before the British started the building on fire.

The net result of this seven hour action was that the rebels had attained their greatest victory of the Easter Rising. Thirteen Volunteers had inflicted over 230 casualties upon the British force at a cost of four dead and one captured.

As an aside, two of the fighters in Clanwilliam House, Tom and Jimmy Walsh (brothers) escaped and managed to get out of Dublin. They remained on the run for weeks after the Rising had ended.

The Battle for Mount Street Bridge

REBEL POSITIONS

25 Northumberland Road	Clanwilliam House	Parochial school
*Michael Malone	*George Reynolds	Patrick J. Doyle
James Grace	Jimmy Doyle	Joseph Clarke
	Tom Walsh	William Christian
	Jim Walsh	_____ McGrath\
	Willie Ronan	
	*Richard Murphy	
	*Patrick Doyle	

*killed in action

Those Volunteers killed at Mount Street Bridge:
Reynolds & Doyle (top), Murphy & Malone (bottom)

Clanwilliam House

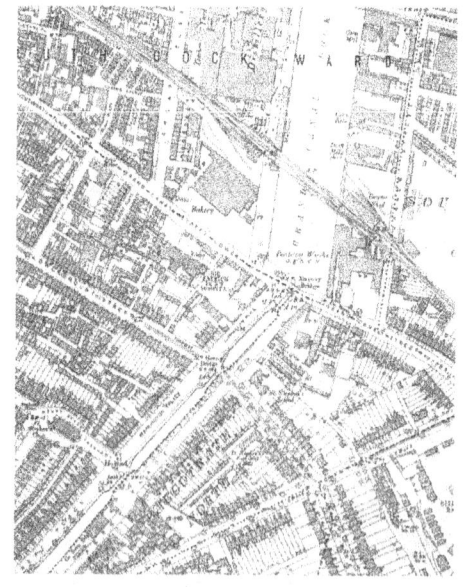

50th Anniversary of the Easter Rising
10 Shilling Coin: Padraig Pearse 1966

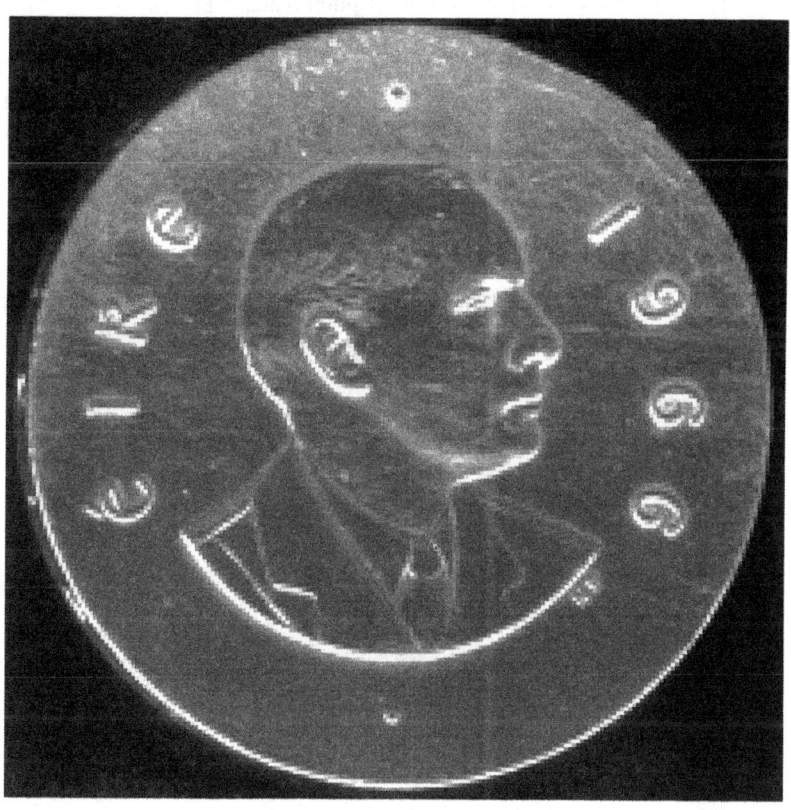

The Irish ten shilling coin was produced for the 50th Anniversary of the Easter Rising in 1966. It is the only modern Irish coin not to feature a sixteen string Irish harp, but rather shows a bust of Patrick Pearse, Commander-in-Chief and head of the Provisional Government.

The coin has Cuchulainn, the ancient Irish hero on the other side. That image is a copy of the statue currently featured in the GPO in Dublin. The value of the coin, 10 shillings, is inscribed in Gaelic as *deich scilling*.

The coin was the only Irish coin to have an edge inscription until the Euro coins were released. The inscription reads: *"Eiri Amach na Casca 1916"* which translates to "1916 Easter Rising".

It was released on April 12, 1966. It contains 83.5% silver and 16.5% copper. Two million were minted, but only 730,000 released as the coin was only popular with collectors. It was officially withdrawn from circulation on February 10, 2002.

Postage Stamps & The Easter Rising

Since independence in 1922 and the formation of the Irish State, the postal authority has issued many postage stamps which note milestone anniversaries of the Easter Rising as well as important dates for the participants.

25th Anniversary of the Easter Rising 1941
(Scott #120)
Volunteer and the GPO
Gaelic words on left are the first words
To the Proclamation

50th Anniversary
1966

50th Anniversary: Death of Roger Casement

Centenary of the Birth of James Connolly

Centenary of the Birth of Patrick Pearse

Centenary of the Birth of Eamonn deValera

Centenary of the Birth of Michael Collins 1990

75th Anniversary 1991

90th Anniversary 2006

Movie Review
"Michael Collins"
1996

This is a 'biopic' produced by Neil Jordan on an extremely controversial topic, particularly within Ireland and Great Britain. If one praises the movie too much, he could be branded and I.R.A. supporter. If one finds the picture despicable, then one might be perceived as a Unionist or an apologist for the existence of the British Empire.

In either case, however, there is no denying the power of the picture. One is presented with a Michael Collins torn between the cold realities of Ireland in the 1920's and a man concerned about his interpersonal relationships. Liam Neeson gives perhaps his most powerful performance in the title role. In my mind, however, Alan Rickman mastered the part of Eamonn deValera, despite the historical inaccurcies. Aiden Quinn has a very important counterbalance to Neeson as Harry Boland, while Julia Roberts is acceptable as Kitty Kiernan. While much of the movie concerns Kitty's struggles between Mick and Harry, that part of the movie is too expansive for Kitty's true role in history.

The movie begins with the end of the Easter Rising, and follows through the Anglo- Irish War, the Treaty dilemma, and ends with Collins' death in the Civil War. The filming is truly outstanding. There are, however, some very serious historical errors.

First and foremost, there is little or no evidence to support the notion that deValera was behind the assassination of Michael Collins. In fact, history suggests that he left the area of Beal na mBlath after quarreling with those who set up the ambush, deValera arguing that killing Collins would result in a very serious error.

Also, the death of Harry Boland shows him being shot escaping out of a sewer in Dublin. Actually, Harry Boland was killed coming out of a hotel well to the north of Dublin.

An especially poignant moment occurs in the movie during "Bloody Sunday" when Collins' Special Unit eliminates the British secret operatives, thus crippling British intelligence in Ireland and in effect, winning Irish freedom. The British retaliation at the game in Croke Park that same afternoon, although graphic, is very accurate.

In every aspect, this is a riveting motion picture. The first ten minutes of the movie regarding the Easter Rising really puts those events into perspective. The movie itself is a good point of departure for anyone interested the basis for 'The Troubles' and for anyone who wishes to understand the Ireland of today.

90th Anniversary Observance
Of the Easter Rising
Sunday, April 16, 2006

After an absence of 36 years, a military parade and commemorative activities were planned, sanctioned and carried out by the government of the Republic of Ireland. These events were the first official recognition of the Easter Rising since 1969 when recognition of 1916 was tantamount to legitimatizing the Irish Republican Army (IRA) and its activities.

The parade began at Dublin Castle, proceeded up Dame Street, crossed the Liffey onto O'Connell Street and stopped at the General Post Office (GPO), site of the headquarters during the Rising at the spot where Patrick Pearse read the Proclamation of the Republic. A re-enactment of that reading took place. From there the parade continued up O'Connell Street to the Garden of Remembrance at the Rotunda Hospital.

Events were also held at Arbour Hill Cemetery and Kilmainham Gaol. The event was attended by more than 100,000 people. Its success is an omen for the type of celebration to be planned for the 100th Anniversary in 2016.

Dublin parade's Easter rising
Ireland to celebrate 1916 rebellion for 1st time in 37 years

Kevin Cullen, Boston Globe
Sunday, March 19, 2006

(03-19) 04:00 PDT Dublin -- Everybody loves a parade, right?

Well, here in Ireland's capital, it depends on whom you ask.

After an absence of 36 years, there will be a military parade here on Sunday, April 16, to commemorate the 90th anniversary of the Easter Rising of 1916. The parade was suspended after widespread conflict broke out in Northern Ireland in the summer of 1969, and the Provisional Irish Republican Army said it was carrying the mantle of the 1916 rebels. The Irish government was loath to do anything that might suggest legitimacy for the IRA, such as a parade celebrating a group that killed people.

These days, with the conflict in the north reduced mainly to one of politics, Prime Minister Bertie Ahern announced last fall that the Easter Rising parade, with full military trappings, would resume. Some accused Ahern of political opportunism. Others say it is obscene to celebrate the fanatical brand of nationalism that inspired the Rising's leaders. Some say it borders on self-loathing for Ireland to ignore its revolutionary roots.

And many others say, hey, chill out, it's only a parade.

For the traveler, however, the attraction of being in Ireland these days is to listen to the debate. And for all the majesty of the Cliffs of Moher, the serene beauty of the lakes of Killarney and the haunting vista of William Butler Yeats's grave under Ben Bulben, there is nothing quite so intriguing as an Irish argument.

The parade will step off from Dublin Castle, the onetime seat of the British administration, which is worth a visit in itself. It will wind down Dame Street, to College Green, before bearing left up O'Connell Street, past the General Post Office, which was rebel headquarters. At the GPO, the Proclamation of Independence will be read out, as the Rising's leader, Padraig Pearse read it to a bewildered few who happened to be about on Easter Monday, at four minutes past noon, after the rebels seized the post office.

The GPO, one of the city's last great Georgian buildings, is worth a visit. Though it is a busy post office, the Rising is its inescapable legacy: Outside, the walls have pockmarks from bullets fired during the five days the rebels held the building; inside, the walls are lined with a series of 10 portraits that show various events during the Rising. Ahern recently announced plans to convert the GPO into a national monument, so its days as a working post office are numbered.

Also worth a visit is Kilmainham Gaol, where 15 of the Rising's leaders were executed by British firing squads. Those executions reversed Irish public opinion, which had initially been opposed to the rebellion, and eventually led to a more popular, more successful revolution that won independence for 26 of Ireland's 32 counties.

But it was what later happened in the other six counties, which make up Northern Ireland, that made the Irish Republic reluctant to celebrate what for the Irish is their battle of Lexington and Concord.

President Mary McAleese, a native of Northern Ireland, touched off controversy in January when she gave a speech suggesting that the Rising gave rise to the affluent, secular and increasingly diverse society that Ireland has become. But she seemed to acknowledge that her speech would provoke arguments throughout Ireland's sitting rooms, kitchens, and pubs.

"In a free and peaceful democracy, where complex things get figured out through public debate, that is as it should be," she said.

EPILOGUE

As we approach the middle of 2007, perhaps it would be wise to reflect upon what has occurred over the past ninety one years. The Easter Rising ignited Irish nationalism, resulting in a victory for independence through the bloody Anglo-Irish War (1919-1921) and the equally traumatic Irish Civil War (1922). What emerged from all of the conflict was certainly not perfect- the ideals of the Easter Rising were not a reality due to the partition of the six counties.

As a result, all the early great leaders of Ireland were lost, Patrick Pearse, Thomas Clarke, James Connolly, Michael Collins, Arthur Griffith, etc. What remained was Eamonn deValera, crafty as a politician and stubborn beyond the patience of his contemporaries. He guided Ireland from 1927 through 1975, during which time the country abrogated many parts of the treaty which was signed in 1921. He maintained Ireland's neutrality during World War II, much to the dismay of England. He was able to change the country from the Irish Free State to the Republic of Ireland, and it may be argued that he laid the foundation (after decades of aloofness) for the origins of the *Celtic Tiger*.

I would be most hesitant to deify deValera and place him in the heroic category as those mentioned above, but he is a fact of history. Also a fact of history are the turbulent years from 1916 to 1923. Everyone can take any side they wish in the debate, treaty/anti-treaty, republican/loyalist, Catholic/Protestant. What has transpired during the past nine decades cannot be altered. The people of Ireland and those who claim Irish heritage must digest history as it is and must also realize that the best interest of Ireland lies in an island nation united towards a better life for its people.

By 2006, Gerry Adams and yes, even Ian Paisley, both came to that realization. Devolution of government for Northern Ireland is the only sane and real step forward for the six counties. Over the next nine years during the run-up to the Centenary of the Easter Rising, people in all thirty two counties will have the opportunity to assimilate the idea of a united Ireland.

The wounds of the Troubles are a generation old currently and they must be healed in the short term. That was the vision of Pearse, Clarke and Connolly, and its realization will finally give true meaning to their sacrifice.

Bibliography

Augusteijn, Joost, *The Irish Revolution 1913-1923*, Pelgrave, Basingstoke, 2002

Barton, Brian, *Secret Court Martial Records 1916*, Blackstaff, Belfast, 2002

Boyle, John, *The Irish Revolution of 1916*, Constable, London, 1916

Brennan-Whitmore, W.J., *Dublin Burning*, Macmillan, Dublin, 1996

Caulfield, Max, *The Easter Rebellion*, Four Square, London, 1963

Coffey, Thomas, *Agony at Easter*, Harrap, London, 1970

Connell, Joseph E.A., Jr., *Where's Where in Dublin*, Dublin City, Dublin, 2006

Coogan, Tim Pat, *1916: The Easter Rising*, Cassell, London, 2001

Coogan, Tim Pat, *deValera: The Long Fellow*, London, 1995

Coogan, Tim Pat, *Ireland in the 20th Century*, Pelgrave, London, 2003

Coogan, Tim Pat, *Michael Collins: The Big Fellow*, Arrow, London, 1990

Coogan, Tim Pat, *Wherever Green is Worn*, Pelgrave, London, 2000

Cordozo, Nancy, *Lucky Eyes & A High Heart*, Bobbs Merrill, New York, 1978

deCourcey, John, *The Sea and The Easter Rising*, Corgi, London, 1991

DeRosa, Peter, *Rebels: The Easter Rising 1916*, Fawcett, New York, 1990

Duff, Charles, *Six Days to Shake an Empire*, Dent, London, 1966

Edwards, Dudley, *1916: The Easter Rising*, MacGibbon, London, 1968

Edwards, Ruth Dudley, *Patrick Pearse: The Triumph of Failure*, Taplinger, New York, 1978

Fitzgerald, Desmond, *Memoirs 1913-1916,* Routledge, London, 1968

Fitzhenry, Edna, *Nineteen Sixteen,* Gill, Dublin, 1935

Fox, R.M., *History of the Irish Citizen Army,* Duffy, Dublin, 1943

Foy, Michael & Brian Barton, *The Easter Rising,* Sutton, London, 2004

Harris, Nathaniel, *The Easter Rising,* Dryad, London, 1987

Hart, Peter, *Mick,* Panmacmillan, London, 2006

Hegarty, Sean & Fintan O'Toole, *The Irish Time: Book of the 1916 Rising,* Gill & Macmillan, Dublin, 2006

Henderson, Frank, *Easter Rising Recollections,* University Press, Cork, 1968

Henry, Fr. OFM Cap., *The Capuchin Annual 1966,* Church Street, Dublin, 1966

Kiberd, Declan (Ed), *1916: The Easter Rebellion Handbook,* Mourne River Press, Dublin, 1998

Killeen, Richard, *The Easter Rising,* Thomas Learning, New York, 1995

Kostick, Conor & Lorcan Collins, *Easter Rising: A Guide to Dublin in 1916,* O'Brien, Dublin, 2000

MacEntee, Sean, *Episode at Easter,* Gill, Dublin, 1966

MacThomais, Eamonn, *Down Dublin Streets 1916,* Irish Book, Dublin, 1965

Maher, Jim, *Harry Boland,* Mercier, Cork, 1998

Marreco, Anne, *The Rebel Countess,* Chilton, London, 1967

Martin, F.X., *The Irish Volunteers,* Duffy, Dublin, 1963

Martin, F.X., *Leaders and Men of the Rising,* Metheun, London, 1967

McCoole, Sinead, *No Ordinary Women,* University of Wisconsin, Madison, 2002

McHugh, Roger, *Dublin 1916*, Arlington, London, 1966

McLoughlin, Dean, *Memories of the Easter Rising 1916*, Camillian, Westmeath, 1948

McMahon, Sean, *Rebel Ireland*, Mercier, Cork, 2006

O'Connor, Frank, *The Big Fellow*, Poolbeg, Dublin, 1965

O'Farrell, Mick, *A Walk in Rebel Dublin*, Mercier, Cork, 1999

O'Higgins, Brian, *The Soldier's Story of Easter Week*, Glasnevin, Dublin, 1925

O'Neill, Brian, *Easter Week*, Lawrence, London, 1936

O'Rahilly, Aodogan, *Winding the Clock*, Liliput, Dublin, 1991

Purdon, Edward, *The Easter Rising*, Mercier, Cork, 1999

Ryan, Annie, *Witnesses: Inside the Easter Rising*, Liberties, Dublin, 2005

Ryan, Desmond, *The Rising*, Golden Eagle, London, 1966

Stephens, James, *The Insurrection in Dublin*, Macmillan, New York, 1916

Taillon, Ruth, *When History Was Made: The Women of 1916*, Beyond the Pale, Dublin, 1996

Townshend, Charles, *Easter 1916: The Irish Rebellion*, Mercier, Cork, 2006

Trimble, David, *The Easter Rebellion of 1916*, Ulster Society, Armagh, 1992

Ward, Alan, *The Easter Rising*, AHM, Illinois, 1980

Ward, Margaret, *Unimaginable Revolutionaries*, University of Michigan, Ann Arbor, 1996

INDEX
(items in bold type indicate a dedicated piece)

1st Volunteer Training Corps 55
2nd King Edward's 55

"A Soldier's Song" 92
Adams, John 56
Allen Thomas 56
Amiens Street Station 45
Arbour Hill Cemetery 9, 50, 68, 78, 142
Arbour Hill Prison 66, 68, 96, 109, 120
Army Service Corps 55
Ashe, Thomas 49
Aud xii, 33, 119

Beaslei, Piaras 63
Beggar's Bush Barracks 44
Bevan, Thomas 62
Blackadder, General 69
Boland's Bakery 24, 33, 34, 36, 37, 41, 85, 124, 130
Boland, Harry 63, 102, 141
Bowen-Colthurst, Capt. 116, 117
Broadstone Station 45
Brown, Nancy 26, 106
Brugha, Cathal 13, **22,** 39, 40, 43, 49, 51, 74, 114, 115
Burke, Frank 56
Byrne, Andrew 56
Byrne James 56
Byrne Joseph 56

Capuchin Annual 1966 73, 91, 107
Capuchin Friars xiv, 71, 107, 109, 118, 119, 120
Carisbrook House 129
Carrigan, Charles 56
Carney, Winifred **30,** 32, 41, 102
Casement, Sir Roger xi, **27,** 49, 51, 137
Ceannt, Eamonn 7, **13,** 16, 22, 34, 39, 40, 43, 49, 69, 109, 114, 115, 121, 136
Christian, William 131

Church Street 18, 35, 41, 107, 108, 109, 110, 121, 123
Citizen's Army **6,** 10, 23, 25, 28, 30, 71, 89, 109, 111, 113, 116, 124
City Hall 30, 33, 34, 35
Clan na Gael 6
Clanwilliam House 35, 38, 129, 130
Clarke, Joseph 130, 131
Clarke, Kathleen (Daly) 9, 67
Clarke, Philip 56
Clarke, Thomas, xi, xii, xiii, 6, 7,**9,** 18, 33, 34, 42, 43, 49, 50, 62, 66, 67, 68, 100, 110, 120, 132, 136, 145
Cathal Brugha Barracks 75, 88
Cogan's Shop 102
Colbert, Con **16,** 43, 49, 63, 69, 71
Coliseum Theatre 100
Collins, Michael xiv, 15, 49, 52, 89, 138, 140, 141, 145
Connolly, James xii, xiii, 7, **10,** 25, 30, 33, 34, 35, 36, 39, 40, 41, 42, 43, 49, 63, 66, 69, 81, 100, 102, 109, 110, 111, 112, 113, 121, 124, 127, 129, 136, 137, 145
Connolly, Sean 56
Corcoran, James 56
Cosgrove, William 63
Costello, John 56
Coughlan, Fr. Leonard OFM Cap. 120, 122, 123
Coyle, Harry 56
Crinigan, John 56
Cromean, John 56
Cuchulainn 133, 134
Cumann na mBann **7,** 25, 71, 108, 124, 125
Czira, Sidney Gifford 94

Dail Eireann 8, 24
Daly, Edward (Ned) 9, **18,** 19, 35, 41, 43, 49, 62, 67, 69, 109
Darcy, Charles 56
Darcy, Peter 56

deValera, Eamonn 8, **24,** 34, 37, 49, 52, 63, 69, 124, 128, 130, 138, 145
Devoy, John 6

Dillon, Thomas 94
Doherty, John 62
Doyle, Jimmy 131
Doyle, Patrick 56, 130, 131
Doyle, Patrick J. 131
Dublin Castle 35, 44, 66, 70, 109, 142
Dublin Metropolitan Police 34, 55
Duffy, Louise Gavan 7 124

Ennis, Edward 56

Farrell, Patrick 56
Father Matthew Hall 71, 107, 108, 109, 123, 124
Fianna Eireann 7, 19, 25, 35, 37, 126
Fianna Fail 24, 25, 128
Fitzgerald, Desmond 100, 105
Flanagan, Fr. 100
Fort Kelly 38
Four Courts 18, 233, 35, 40, 41, 44, 46, 85, 109
Fox, James 56
Fr. Albert OFM Cap. 69, 71, 107, 108, 110, 120, 121, 123
Fr. Aloysius OFM Cap. 69, 71, 107, 108, 110, 121, 123
Fr. Augustine OFM Cap. 69, 71, 107, 108, 110, 120, 121, 123
Fr. Jarlath OFM Cap. 108
Fr. Sebastian OFM Cap. 69, 107, 108, 110, 123

Gaelic League 12, 13, 20, 22, 24
General Post Office (GPO) xiv, 12, 21, 26, 30, 32, 33, 34, 36, 37, 38, 39, 40, 41, 44, 46, 85, 90, 94, 100, 102, 105, 113, 129, 135, 139, 142
Geoghegan, George 56
Gifford, Grace (Plunkett) 15, **31,** 43, 69, 93, 94, 102
Gifford, Muriel 94
Glasnevin Cemetery 27, 119, 128

Gonne, Maud (MacBride) 17, 53, 94, 125
"Grace" 31, 98
Grace, James 129, 131
Grenan, Julia 32, 41, 102
Griffith, Arthur vix, 8, 94 104, 145
Haddington Road 38
Hanlon's Fish Shop 42, 102
Harcourt Street Station 45
Healy, John 56
Heaney, Patrick 92
Helga 37
Heuston, Sean 18, **19,** 35, 37, 38, 43, 49, 63, 68, 69, 71, 121
Hobson, Bulmer xi, 7, 104
Howard, Sean 56
Hunter, Thomas 63
Hurley, John 56
Hussars 55

Inghinidhe na hEreann 126
Irish Brigade
Irish Free State
Irish Parliamentary Party
Irish Republican Brotherhood (IRB) 6, 7, 11, 12, 24, 15, 28, 33, 104, 105
Irish Republican Army **8,** 142
Irish Volunteers **7,** 11, 13, 14, 26, 27, 119, 124
Irish Transport & General Workers Union xiii, 6, 10, 110
Irvine, George 62

Jacob's Biscuit Factory 11, 17, 20, 33, 35, 36, 41, 44, 85, 94, 109
Jamison Distillery 16, 34
Jervis Street Hospital 41

Kealy, John 56
Kearney, Peadar 49, 92
Kent, Edmund 63
Kent, Richard 56
Kent, Thomas 63
Keogh, Margueretta 124
Keogh, Richard 56
Kiernan, Kitty 140
Kilmainham Gaol xiv, 9, 10, 11, 12, 13, 14, 15, 16, 17, 18, 19, 20,

21, 23, 67,69, 78, 95, 110, 120, 127, 142
Kingsbridge Station 19, 36 45
King Street North 18, 35, 41, 71, 108

Lancers 55
Leacheaky, John 95
Leinster Regiment 55
Liberty Hall xii, 33, 37, 48, 105, 112, 113
Linenhall Barracks 44
Lockout of 1913 xiii, 6, 25, 111, 116, 126
Lowe, General 32, 35, 36, 42
Lynch, Diarmuid 102
Lynch, Finian 62
Lynn, Dr. Kathleen **30**

MacBride, John **17,** 43, 49, 63, 68, 69, 109
MacBride, Sean 17
MacDonagh, Thomas xi, 7, **11,** 20, 35, 43, 49, 62, 66, 67, 68, 81, 94, 109, 110, 111, 120, 136
Macken, Peter 56
Macken, Peter 56
MacNeill, Eoin xi, 7, 26, 32, 33, 63, 104, 105
Mallin, Michael 6, **23,** 34, 36, 43, 49, 63, 68, 69, 120, 127
Mallin, Una 120
Mahoney, George 100
Malone, Michael 56, 129, 130, 131
Manning, Peter 56
Marlborough Barracks 37, 44
Markievicz, Casimir 126
Markievicz, Constance (Gore-Booth)
7, 23, **25,** 34, 49, 53, 63, 678, 69, 94, 120, 124, 125, 126, 127, 128
Maxwell, Sir John **29,** 40, 42, 43, 66, 69
McCarthy, Fr. Eugene 95
McCormack, J 56
McDermott, Sean 6, 7, **14,** 42, 43, 49, 63, 69, 100, 110, 121, 136
McNestry, Patrick 62
M'Dowell, William 56

Mendicity Institution 19, 33, 35, 37, 74
Mervyn, Michael 62
Military Council IRB xi, 7, 9, 10, 12, 13, 14, 17, 33, 36, 128
Moira House 74
Mount Street Bridge 33, 38, 44, 47, 85, 129, 130, 131
Murphy, Fr. Columbus 107
Murphy, D 56
Murphy, Richard 57, 130, 131
Murray, D 57

Naval Detachment 55
North Dublin Union 108
North King Street
North Stratfordshires 55
Northumberland Road #25 25, 28, 48, 129

O'Callaghhan, Dennis 62
O'Carroll, Richard 57
O'Farrell, Agnes 7, 124
O'Farrell, Elizabeth **32,** 41, 42, 102, 125
O'Flanagan, Peter 57
O'Grady, John 57
O'Hanrahan, Michael **20,** 43, 62, 67, 69
O'Meara, Frank 98
O'Meara Sean 98
O'Rahilly, Michael (The) xi, 7, **26,** 40, 49, 53, 57, 100, 102, 104, 105, 106, 112
O'Rahilly, Aodogan 106
O'Reilly, J 57
O'Reilly, Richard 57
O'Reilly, Thomas 57
Owens, J 5Paisley, Rev. Ian 145

Pearse, Margaret 117
Pearse,Patrick xi, xiii, 6, 7, 11, **12,** 16, 18, 21 ,29 ,30 ,32 ,33 ,34 ,36, 41 ,42, 43, 49, 62, 66, 67, 68, 70, 81, 94, 100, 102, 104, 109, 110, 120, 121, 122, 123, 125, 133, 134, 136, 137, 142, 145
Pearse, William **21,** 43, 49, 62, 67, 69, 94
Pembroke Road 38

Plunkett, Count 94
Plunkett, George 63
Plunkett, Geraldine 94
Plunkett, John 63
Plunkett, Joseph 7, **15,** 31, 43, 49, 62, 67, 69, 93, 94, 100, 102, 111, 131
Portobello Barracks 35, 44, 114, 116,
Prisoners 64

Quinn, James 57

Rafferty, Thomas 57
Reid, J.J. 62
Reilly's Fort 41
Reynolds, George 57, 130, 131
Richmond Barracks 12, 16, 36, 44, 66, 67, 71, 78, 81, 84
Richmond Hospital 108, 124
Roana, Willie 131
Robbins, Frank 75
Rotunda Hospital 42, 66
Royal Barracks 37, 44
Royal College of Surgeons 23, 35, 34, 36, 41, 124, 127
Royal Field Artillery 55
Royal Hospital Kilmainham 36, 37
Royal Inniskilling Fusiliers 55
Royal Irish Constabulary 55
Royal Irish Fusiliers 55
Royal Irish Regiment 55
Royal Irish Rifles 55
Ryan, Frank 57

St. Mary's Church- Haddington Road 130
St. Stephen's Green 6, 23, 25, 33, 34, 35, 44, 85, 124
St. Stephen's Parochial School 129
Sheehan, Domhnall 57
Sheehy-Skeffington, Francis 21, **28,** 43, 116
Sheehy-Skeffington, Hanna
Shelbourne Hotel 34, 36
Sherwood Foresters 38, 55, 129
Ship Street Barracks 44
Sinn Fein xiv, **8,** 24, 26, 104, 126
Smith, John 95

South Dublin Union 13, 16, 22, 33, 34, 36, 39, 40, 41, 44, 74, 85, 109, 117
South Stratfordshire 55
Stephens, James 6
Stonebreaker's Yard 16, 68, 69
Sweeney, P.E. 62

Tobin (Surgeon) 69
Tobin, William 62
Traynor, John 57
Trinity College 36, 38

U-19 119
Ulster Volunteers
United Irish League 46

Volunteers xi, 15, 16, 20, 24, 33, 71, 89, 104

Wadkin's Brewery 16, 34
Walsh, Edward 57
Walsh, JJ 62, 130, 131
Walsh, Thomas 62, 130, 131
Weafer, Thomas 57
Wellington Barracks 44, 71
Westland Row Station 35, 45
Whelan, Patrick 57
Wheeler, Capt.
Williams, John 63
Wyse-Power, Jennie 7, 124

Yeomanry 55

www.ingramcontent.com/pod-product-compliance
Lightning Source LLC
Chambersburg PA
CBHW070918180426
43192CB00038B/1754